Children on Consignment

CHILDREN ON CONSIGNMENT

A Handbook for Parenting Foster Children and Their Special Needs

by

PHILIP MICHAEL STAHL

Lexington Books

D.C. Heath and Company • Lexington, Massachusetts • Toronto

Library of Congress Cataloging-in-Publication Data

Stahl, Philip Michael.
Children on consignment : a handbook for parenting foster children
and their special needs / by Philip Michael Stahl.
p.   cm.
ISBN 0-669-21841-3 (alk. paper)
1. Foster children—United States. 2. Parenting—United States.
3. Parent and child—United States. 4. Foster children—United
States—Family relationships.   I. Title.
HV875.55.S73   1990
362.7'33'0973—dc20   90-5765
                                                                         CIP

Published simultaneously in Canada
Printed in the United States of America
International Standard Book Number: 0-669-21841-3
Library of Congress Catalog Card Number: 90-5765

The paper used in this publication meets the minimum requirements of
American National Standard for Information Sciences—Permanence
of Paper for Printed Library Materials, ANSI Z39.48-1984.

Year and number of this printing:

90 91 92 93 94 8 7 6 5 4 3 2 1

To Andrea, Jason, and Rebecca. You have provided me the love, support, and the time, while being there through all of my work.

Contents

Preface

OVER the last fifteen years, I have spent much of my professional life working with children and families in foster care. During that time, I have seen a rise in the number of children in foster care that has been incredible. Currently in the United States, there are nearly 500,000 children in foster homes and institutions. This represents a 25 percent increase in only the past four years. In California alone, there are nearly 64,000 children in foster homes, more than twice the number ten years ago. While the number of teens in care tends to remain stable, the number of foster children aged seven to fourteen is growing at a steady rate, and the growing number of children under age seven in care is staggering.

Rampant drug use is the primary cause of this. Reports suggest that nearly one baby in ten is currently born with an illegal substance in its body. Many children are sexually abused and come into care with sexually transmitted diseases. The mental health of these children is severely affected by the disorganized homes in which they live, and by the assault on their minds and bodies while in the care of their biological parents.

During the last fifteen years, the most common complaint that I have heard has been that foster parents are not treated as professionals and do not receive sufficient training for their work. Society gives children to foster parents "on consignment," and these parents have a great opportunity to help their foster children. This book is addressed to foster parents, and its purpose is to help them better understand the needs of their foster children and to provide them with parenting techniques that are most effective in dealing with a variety of problems that foster children normally have.

A key to understanding all children is the recognition that their behaviors and needs change according to their age. Most parents find it relatively easy to understand children of a particular age but feel somewhat confused by the same children when they are older. This problem is worse for foster parents, who typically haven't lived with the child since birth. The bonds between foster parent and foster child are different, and it always requires an adjustment for foster parents whenever a new child comes into the house.

Another key to understanding all children is to recognize that their behaviors—especially their misbehaviors—are often the result of feelings that the children keep inside. Foster children often come into foster homes with a variety of "negative" feelings that they don't understand. These feelings cause most of the misbehaviors in foster children, especially in younger ones.

It is my hope that this book can provide foster parents with the understanding necessary to build a foundation for raising children in foster care. By understanding these children's developmental, emotional, and behavioral needs, and by taking a look at their own expectations about foster parenting, foster parents can continue their efforts to achieve the goal of professionalism in foster care.

Acknowledgments

T HIS book is the result of much of my professional work. In 1976, as a relatively inexperienced psychologist, I began to evaluate foster children who were living in temporary shelters while awaiting more "permanent" foster placement. Little did I know it at that time, but the words *permanent* and *foster placement* do not go together. Through the years, I saw and learned a great deal about foster care from everyone I worked with in the foster care system.

Professionally, I owe a great deal to the large and dedicated foster care staff of the Wayne County (Michigan) Department of Social Services, who first introduced me to the problems of foster children. While I was consulting with them indirectly, I also worked directly with Lutheran Social Services of Michigan, and it was while I worked with them that the ideas for this book were first developed. In nearly every staff meeting, we discussed the problem behaviors of the children and the parenting issues of their foster parents. I asked my colleagues if there were books on the subject that we could recommend to the foster parents. We looked for some, but we recognized that there were none. That realization led me to this project. Thus, the staff of Lutheran Social Services, both directly and indirectly, enabled me to recognize the need for this project and initially assisted me in addressing the issues that this book addresses.

In my subsequent work in California, two foster parents have been especially helpful to me in this project. Margaret Woodard and Diane Humbert (both of Alameda County, California) were kind enough to review very rough manuscripts and provide me with ideas and encouragement along the way. My uncle, Harry Ingram, assisted me with early editing, and a variety of people, especially Linda Permut, helped me type the various initial drafts.

My family also assisted me greatly with their patience and encouragement, and I am sure that they will be pleased when I no longer have to say "I've got to get back to working on my book." Without all their help, this book could not have been completed.

Finally, I owe a special debt of gratitude to all the foster children I have known in the last fourteen years. I have learned a lot from all of you about love, patience, understanding, and the ability of the human spirit to endure hardship. Each of you, in some way, has touched my heart, and I only hope I've been able to find a way to help you understand yourselves better as you continue your own journeys through life. Whether our contact was brief, in an evaluation, or more lengthy, in therapy, you have helped me to understand the importance of relationships in life and how fragile they can be. By working together to bring real permanence into your lives, both as children and in adulthood, all of us can help change a system that needs much change. Thank you for letting me hear your pain, and see your joy, in whatever we have done together.

Children on Consignment

1

Introduction and Philosophy

YOU have decided to become a foster parent! But all of a sudden, you are not quite sure why you have chosen to do this or how to do it effectively. You know that you love children and have a lot to offer children with special needs, and you are determined to be the best foster parent you possibly can. But perhaps doubts linger because you are not quite sure what this is going to be like. Maybe you have already had a couple of children of your own, or maybe you have been around children long enough to have some ideas about parenting. But parenting someone else's children is going to be different. The purpose of this book is to help explain how and why foster children come into care, and to help foster parents understand some of the special needs that they are asked to work with on a daily basis.

People choose to become foster parents for a variety of reasons. Most foster parents are recruited either by foster care agencies or by other foster parents. Recruiters and other foster parents talk about the insufficiency of good foster homes for children who have been abused and neglected by their biological parents and who have nowhere to live. As such, a sense of goodwill and a desire to help children are major components in the choice to become a foster parent. Most adults who become foster parents like children, feel they have a lot to give children, and truly believe that they can provide the temporary love and care that foster children need.

In addition, like all other choices adults make, this choice frequently involves many other motives. Some adults have personally known children who required the help of foster parents. Others were raised by foster parents themselves during part of their own childhood. Still other adults have a *need* to help take care of others, believing that is their duty in life. For some of them, this involves religious beliefs, while for others, it is more emotionally based. Some adults see foster parenting as a way to supplement their income, or as a source of extra spending money for a family, as well as a chance to perform a useful function. Some adults have wanted biological children but are unable to have them, and they choose foster parenting to temporarily fill their need to take care of children. Often, such parents hope to ultimately adopt the child they are fostering. Some foster parents are recruited for one situation only, for infants or young children whose parents are considered likely to have their parental rights terminated, leaving their children available for adoption by foster parents. Foster parents' other motives may be a need for companionship for themselves or their children or a need to possibly "replace" children who have grown and moved out of the home. Some adults feel a need to rescue children who are in need, and foster parenting is a way to do this. Understanding their own motives may assist foster parents in becoming the responsible and effective foster parent that they hope to be.

Foster Parent Home Studies

Early in the recruitment process, the potential foster parents are interviewed by a social service agency in what is known as a home study. While some questions asked in this interview may appear to be intrusive, prospective foster parents should know that all the questions are designed to help ensure the safety of the children. Social workers are required by the state to guarantee the safety of children who come under their jurisdiction. Only by doing complete and thorough evaluation of prospective foster parents can they ensure that children who have been at risk because of abuse or neglect will have a better experience in foster care.

There are many characteristics that social workers look for in evaluating foster parent capacity. The questions social workers ask in the home study enable them to obtain information about prospective parents' daily routine, their work experience, their relationships with friends and family, and other day-to-day aspects of their lives. It is important to know how the prospective foster parents deal with anger, sadness, frustration, and the like. It is important to know about their ability to resolve conflicts and crises. Since foster parenting is sometimes very difficult, questions are asked about the parents' ability to remain committed to a difficult task. Questions about foster parents' dependency on social services or their ability to utilize other supports (friends and family) are also frequently asked. There are questions about the role the foster child will take within the family and how the child will be a part of the family. There are questions about the foster parents' motivations, and how these motives might relate to their ability to meet the child's needs. There are likely questions about how the foster child will affect other children in the home, or the marital or dating relationships. In addition, there are questions about how open the foster parents may be in dealing with the biological parents and about how the foster parents will handle the child's frequent need to talk about his past. In particular, there are direct questions about parent management skills, about the prospective parents' knowledge of child development, and their knowledge of disciplinary techniques and which ones were used on the prospective parents when they themselves were children. Clearly, there are questions about whether the applicants use alcohol or drugs or have a history of criminal activities or other things that could obviously endanger the child.

These questions are designed not only to gather factual information but to help determine which prospective parents will be more responsive to children's needs and more comfortable taking risks, which will remain committed to a difficult task, which will deal effectively with children's emotions, and which have healthy relationship skills and positive relationship capacity. An ability to deal openly and effectively with feelings is also essential. Finally, foster parents need to have good problem-solving skills that they can use when they are confronted with difficulties.

After prospective foster parents have gone through the home study and have been accepted as foster parents, they undergo some initial foster parent training. This training usually includes discussions on the developmental needs of children and on how and why children come into care, and most important, on the licensing rules and regulations of the state in which the foster parents reside.

In addition, the training includes discussions about the typical problems of foster children and the interrelationships between the people involved in the foster care "system." In general, after the prospective parents are accepted as foster parents and have gone through their initial training, they await placement of a child in their home with the expectation that they will be very good foster parents.

The rest of this chapter will focus on the foster care system and how children become part of it, and on the concept of being a "good enough" foster parent. The rest of the book addresses the special needs and problems of foster children and how foster parents can best meet these needs.

What Is Foster Care?

Foster care is a program designed to provide a child who needs care with a substitute family life experience in a household for either a temporary or an extended period of time. This becomes necessary either because the biological family is nonexistent or because that family has significant problems of a social, emotional, economic, and/or physical nature. Foster care was established in the belief that all children have a right to physical, educational, and emotional care, and if biological parents are unable to provide it, foster parents can be recruited to do so.

Foster care provides a healthy home and community experience for a child away from the family. Foster care is expected to be temporary, and a primary goal of foster care is to work toward permanent placement for the child. Thus, while the child is in foster care, it is determined whether her best interests is to return to her biological family or to enter another situation, such as adoption, permanent foster care, or residential treatment.

Essentially, it is a foster family's responsibility to provide twenty-four-hour nurturing care to the child. Foster parents have a responsibility to help the child develop a good self-image and gain positive feelings about his past, present, and future. While the foster parents are the primary participants in this process, the social service agency, the biological parents, and the community at large also contribute to the overall welfare of the foster child.

Ultimately, the court also plays a major role in this system as well, since a judge makes the final determination about both temporary and permanent plans for the child. Thus, the foster care system needs to be seen in its entirety, and the foster parents' responsibilities as part of this whole. The foster parents' responsibilities may be the most critical part in that they are the ones who provide the day-to-day security, support, and nurturance that the child may need to help overcome the problems associated with his past.

How Children Come into the Foster Care System

Foster care has changed a great deal over the past thirty years. Before the 1960s, many children came into foster care when their parents died, or they came from orphanages or other group home environments. At that time, only a small number of children were placed in foster homes as a result of abuse or neglect. But more recently, as states have begun to investigate and pass more comprehensive laws regarding child neglect and abuse, the foster care system has been developed in greater detail. Today, thousands of children enter the foster care system in cities across the United States every year, most often as the result of the economic, physical, social, and/or emotional problems of their parents (such as abusive or neglectful behavior). Foster children range in age from birth through eighteen, but the majority are of school age. While the average age of foster children in the United States is approximately twelve and a half years, more and more children are coming into foster care who are younger than this. Today, a large number of drug-dependent babies are coming into the system from birth, and even more infants and toddlers come into foster care as a result of massive abuse or neglect suffered at the hands of their drug-abusing parents.

Abused children come to the attention of social service agencies and the courts through school reports, through reports of physicians and mental health personnel, through neighbors or relatives who have firsthand knowledge of a problem, or through other people whom most states require to report "suspicion" of child abuse or neglect. Since most states have laws about child abuse reporting, more and more families are being referred to the social service system, which ultimately leads more children into foster care.

Some cases of neglect are relatively mild and are related to economic conditions within the family. But other cases of neglect are more severe, such as keeping a child home from school, leaving a child under age twelve alone for hours or days at a time with no supervision, or generally being either physically or psychologically absent from a child's life. Most states provide that neglected children are to be removed from their biological homes, but usually only the most pervasive and obviously neglectful situations result in a child being removed and placed in foster care. Most typically, where neglect occurs, a social service agency works with the family to help reduce the poverty level and provide resources that enable the parents to meet the physical and sometimes psychological needs of the child. Thus, while charges of neglect are not that uncommon, the actual removal of a child from home due to neglect alone is fairly rare.

Sometimes parents themselves request placement because they recognize their own inability to cope with their child's demands and needs. This kind of placement is known as "voluntary." But voluntary placement is fairly rare. More often, the parents' own problems prevent them from agreeing to this. At such times, court intervention may be necessary, resulting in an "involuntary" placement.

Most of the children who come into the foster care system do so as a result of child abuse charges. In fact, the increased publicity about child abuse of late and the increased reporting of child abuse make it more likely that the courts will remove children from their homes in order to protect them from potential harm. As drug and alcohol abuse increases, children are exposed to increasingly higher risks of abuse and neglect. The courts are likely to weigh these interactive factors in determining whether children should be removed from home and placed in foster care. Data support the fact that abuse is actually growing and that more children are actually the victims of abuse, but there is also speculation that more and more people are reporting abuse (coincident with the passing state abuse reporting laws), and social service agencies and the courts are enforcing child abuse laws more vigorously than in previous years.

Many professionals—including teachers, school principals, physicians, nurses, social workers, psychologists, and others who are in direct contact with children and their families—are required by state laws to report "suspicion" of child abuse. In most jurisdictions, *abuse* is defined as any physical behavior on the part of adults that leaves bruises on a child's body, or any behavior on the part of adults that endangers the safety or the life of the child. As in cases of neglect, in many of the milder cases of abuse, agencies work with families to try to repair the abuse patterns and to develop more positive methods of discipline that are less damaging to the child. If these efforts fail and minor allegations of abuse are repeated, the child is placed into care as a protective measure. In other instances, however, the abuse is greater, and even so pervasive that the child is immediately removed from his or her family. Symptoms of greater abuse may include serious burns, broken bones, or other physical problems. Recent years have seen an increase in the reporting of sexual abuse, and an increasingly large proportion of children coming into foster care have been sexually abused. Sexual abuse has received a great deal of publicity in the past five years, and the courts are now quicker to remove children from environments in which they are perceived as potential or actual victims of sexual abuse. Sexual abuse is commonly thought of as rape and molestation, but many professionals also regard the exposure of children to inappropriate sexualized behavior as a form of sexual abuse.

Finally, a large group of children come into foster care as a result of a massive interaction of both abuse and neglect. In their homes, they receive little or no parenting, they are essentially psychologically neglected, and they are often physically abused as well. It is in these homes that there is the greatest amount of substance abuse, alcoholism, prostitution, blatant sexuality, and similar problems that leave the parents essentially incapable of parenting. Most often, these children do not come to the attention of social service agencies until their school years. In the meantime, there is for many years a massive amount of neglect and abuse, which the foster parents are then asked to deal with. Children from families in which there is a combination of chaos, abuse, neglect, often substance abuse and/or sexual abuse have the most problems in foster care. To some degree, all foster children have special needs, but children from these more chaotic backgrounds have the most pressing needs and pose the most difficult problems for foster parenting.

Children on Consignment

The foster care experience has no real correlation with any other experience in life. When a family adopts a child, she immediately becomes an integrated part of the family and the family knows that for the rest of her life, their relationship with her will grow and mature and a new family unit will evolve. Similarly, the increasing incidence of blended families has brought a shift in the types of families to which people are becoming accustomed. But unless an adoption breaks or a divorce follows the change of family structure, the expectation is that the newly evolving family will continue.

By contrast, however, foster care is expected to be only temporary, and part of the foster parents' job is to help the child maintain psychological ties with his biological parents. As such, foster children are "on consignment" to the foster parents, awaiting a possible return home. Like a coat on a rack in a store or a piece of work in an art gallery, the foster child is temporarily waiting for another change that will hopefully lead to more permanent stability in his life. Often the child does return to the biological family, but all too frequently foster children are moved from one foster home to another for no apparent reason. In even more serious cases, when parental ties are terminated by the court and the child is made available for adoption, she waits in the foster home for a move to a "permanent" adoptive family. In all these instances, the foster child remains in a temporary—and hence insecure—position within the foster family.

Foster parents are encouraged to support the child's psychological ties with his biological parents. But since foster parents almost always provide a more stable environment than the biological parents did, it is natural for children to become attached to the foster parents. In fact, this attachment is necessary for good parenting. Without such attachment, foster children cannot feel a part of the family enough to follow rules, learn in school, and function reasonably well in the home and community. It is often very difficult for foster parents to nurture the dual attachments the child needs to succeed in foster care. In fact, the children who adjust most easily to foster care are precisely those who are most willing to give up their attachment to their biological parents while in foster care. This may occur even while the child maintains visits with the biological parents and even when she knows she is likely to return home. All this is hard on foster children, but it also makes foster parents more likely to feel trapped between the mixed loyalties of the child.

Foster parents often seem to be the ones who foster the biological parents of their foster children as well as the children. It is common for foster parents to assist the biological parents in developing a rapport with their children during visits, and foster parents frequently become a support for biological parents who are struggling with the fact that their child is in foster care.

Rules and regulations of state licensing agencies may also hinder the attachment of a child within a foster home. In most "intact" families, children develop friendships and spend overnight visits with friends away from home. But many licensing rules prevent this for children in foster homes. Foster parents must also gain agency or the biological parents' permission before taking a foster child out of town, which interferes with spur-of-the-moment vacation plans. Foster parents must take foster children to medical appointments, therapy appointments, and the like, and they have only limited legal rights and limited psychological rights in relation to their foster children. These and similar factors contribute to the sense that a foster child is "on consignment" rather than a "regular" member of the family.

This sense of being on consignment creates additional instability and insecurity for the relationship between the foster child and the foster parents. Thus, the foster care process itself may add to the foster parents' difficulty with their roles and responsibilities. But knowing this in advance and establishing plans ahead of time can reduce the negative effects of the process and allow the foster parents to enhance their relationship with their foster child.

Being a "Good Enough" Foster Parent

Although foster parents choose foster parenting for a variety of reasons, most wish to be the "best" foster parents they can. They recognize that foster children have had numerous problems before coming into foster care, and they want to provide corrective experience for the child. But this attitude toward perfection often leads to "burnout" or to interaction problems between foster parents and foster children. Ultimately, foster parents may begin to wonder why they ever got into foster parenting in the first place. To avoid these complications, it may be healthier for foster parents to approach their foster parenting with the idea of being "good enough" parents rather than "perfect" parents.

The concept of a "good enough" parent that has entered the psychological literature over the past few years essentially acknowledges that parents cannot be "perfect." It acknowledges that while many choices must be made as part of parenting, choices are rarely either "all good" or "all bad." Most parents would like to make all the right choices in their parenting, but it is impossible to do so. If this is true for parenting in general, it is even truer for foster parenting. Since foster parenting is complicated by problems with previous attachments, the child's past history, and the temporary nature of foster care, there are fewer instances in which foster parents can make either clearly "right" or "wrong" choices.

By utilizing the principles of being a "good enough" parent, foster parents can weigh the various options and choices that are available to them and make more informed decisions regarding their foster children. Freed from the burden of always making the "perfect" choice, foster parents can relax and take a calmer approach to their task. As long as foster parents remember that their job is to provide a corrective experience for their foster child and not to undo the effects of the child's history of abuse and neglect, they can do a more satisfying job and have more confidence in their parenting ability.

The main principles of being a "good enough" foster parent are to provide nurturance, positive discipline, structure, and a supportive environment, and to attempt to understand and respond to the foster child's emotions and feelings. Paying attention to the foster child's feelings in both words and actions will give him a sense of being heard and understood, possibly for the first time in his life. This in and of itself is very nurturing to a child. Other, more obvious nurturance includes providing food, pleasurable activities, warmth, and a sense of belonging to a family. The foster care environment is considered supportive if the child can feel at home in the family and be part of the family. The foster home is more supportive if it is more structured and if the foster child can count on meals, bedtime, homework time, playtime, and the like on a regularly scheduled, structured basis. Finally, if discipline is generally positive, utilizing techniques of structure, consistency, and positive reinforcement, a foster child can feel even more supported. Since foster children often come from environments with either harsh punishments or no punishments, a positive disciplinary approach is foreign to them but is helpful in overcoming the negative effects of their past.

With such an approach, foster parents can begin to work toward a healthier relationship with their foster child. With a relaxed approach, foster parent burnout is less likely than when foster parents feel they are working too hard with little or no reward. By working to be "good enough" rather than "perfect" foster parents, they can reduce burnout, have a more positive approach to the problems that occur, and solve problems before things get out of hand. The foster parent training mandated in many states and counties is often insufficient to ensure that the foster parents are "good enough." In the following chapters, we will deal specifically with a number of problems that occur in foster care and look toward ways these problems can most easily and appropriately be resolved.

2

Preparing for the Foster Child

BEFORE a foster child is placed in a foster home, the foster family must comply with local regulations regarding bedroom space, furniture, and so on. The number of children in a bedroom, the number of foster children that can live in a given licensed home, and other items are often limited by licensing rules and regulations. These requirements are discussed with foster parents when they apply for their foster care license.

Foster families must also take into consideration their own needs and requirements and think through how the foster child will relate to them. Foster parents must recognize how their own biological children may feel about the changes that must be made to accommodate the foster child, and it is helpful if foster families can discuss among themselves the changes that they expect fostering to bring about. Families might want to consider how a foster child could affect sleeping habits, mealtimes, recreation, housework, and schoolwork as they brainstorm these ideas. It is important for foster families to keep in mind that they are unlikely to be able to predict all the possible effects of the foster child's placement. But exploring family members' feelings can help prepare them for the changes that *will* occur, and the anxieties both of members of the foster family and of the foster child can be minimized.

When a foster child first arrives, it is important to allow him to adjust gradually to the new environment, primarily because of the anxiety usually inherent in moving into a foster home. He will initially feel like a stranger. By providing him with a sense of welcome and an opportunity to get comfortable in his new environment, his and the family's initial anxieties can be reduced. While families cannot be expected to make major changes in their lifestyle to accommodate the foster child, flexibility can help to ensure a more positive beginning to foster care.

There are many concrete things that a family can do to show this flexibility. For example, the child can be included in decisions regarding meals, the placement of bedroom furniture, choice of TV shows, rearrangement of household chores, and the like. The addition of a foster child means less space for everyone and a need for more sharing of things and places. If either a family member or the foster child has a favorite spot to ride in the car, for example, this needs to be acknowledged and dealt with. There is likely to be more rushing around in the morning to get to school, and more problems sharing bathrooms and eating space. Foster families can prepare for these changes ahead of time and, together with the foster child, learn to accommodate to one another. Including foster children in such "family" decisions makes them feel welcome and helps them adjust more easily to foster families.

Foster children have a right to expect equal treatment within the family. The foster child has her own unique personality and set of behaviors, while the family has its own customs and habits as well. Since the addition of the foster child affects relationships within the family and all their daily routines, planning ahead can help reduce the tensions that this can create. If changes and adjustments occur gradually, if the foster family is flexible and tolerant, and if the family makes the child feel welcome and included in "family" discussions, a new balance is likely to be achieved that will benefit both the foster child and the foster family.

Finally, it is important for foster families to clearly understand the costs of fostering before they take on a foster child. Financially, fostering is typically a "break-even" experience, and foster families must often be prepared to use their own money to feed and clothe the foster child, at least until they are reimbursed by the state or county. The expectations between the foster family and the agency about what the agency will and will not pay for must be clear. Oftentimes, foster families must pay for school supplies and enter-

tainment expenses if a foster child is going to share the same benefits as the foster family's own children. It is important to keep in
mind that foster children expect and need to be treated equally,
and that there needs to be equality in both the quality and the
quantity of what is offered to both the foster child and the foster
family's "own children."

Rules, Consistency, and Structure

Many foster children have difficulty adjusting to foster care because in their primary homes, there was chaos, inconsistency, and
insecurity. Some neglected children do not know when or if they
will be fed; their bedtime is very erratic; or they are not sent to
school regularly. Abused children often fear physical violence, and
they may think that punishment or discipline could come at any
time, without their knowing what form it might take. One of the
important tasks of foster parenting is to provide an environment
that helps the child overcome the negative effects of this inconsistency, insecurity, and abuse or neglect.

The easiest way to begin this is to develop regular patterns
within the home on which the child can depend. These patterns
include regular mealtimes and bedtimes. Children who have been
neglected often hoard food because they fear they might not get
another meal when they are hungry. Providing a regular and consistent mealtime schedule helps these children reduce their fears
as they feel more secure in the knowledge that their next meal will
come at a fixed time. If breakfast is always available soon after
awakening and if lunch and dinner are at generally regular times,
the child's insecurity can be reduced. Providing regular snack times
and a sense of freedom about what to eat often helps reduce battling over food, a frequent source of power struggles in foster homes.

Bedtime is another frequent source of tension in foster care.
Again, in their biological homes, it is quite common that abused
and neglected children have very inconsistent bedtime schedules.
Parents are responsible for putting children to bed, but if they are
not responsive to their children's needs, the children may stay
up very late at night, get very little sleep, and develop an inconsis-

tent sleep pattern that is difficult to readjust. The child may be tired at school, wander the house at night, or have other symptoms of disturbed sleep. Their degree of emotional trauma may cause many foster children to have nightmares. Nightmares can also be caused by the violence they may have experienced, the separation and anxiety of being away from home, or general sleep disturbance. Foster children thus often find it very difficult to go to bed, and they may become very manipulative and demanding at night. It may be hard for them to shift their sleep habits to fit into a "normal" family pattern.

The most successful way to combat sleep problems is to give the child a structured sleep pattern. The more chaotic her experience before foster care, the greater her need for a very structured, routine pattern in foster care. Specifically, having a set, unchanged bedtime, with routines that lead to a relaxation and reduction of activity, will help her reorient herself to a more stable, typical sleep pattern.

Implementation of such a plan could go as follows. First, discuss with the child a regular bedtime. For a youngster in the later elementary years, bedtime might be nine or nine-thirty. For a child who is used to staying up very late, a slightly later bedtime might mean a less drastic shift in the sleep pattern. The consistency of the bedtime, however, is the critical issue. If bedtime is set at nine-thirty, it should be nine-thirty through both the week and the weekend, except in unusual circumstances.

Approximately forty-five minutes before bedtime, a routine pattern should develop in which the child prepares for bed in the same way every night. The purpose of this preparation is to reduce activity, relax the body, and reduce manipulation and battling between the parents and the child. This routine might include a bath or a shower, which is physically relaxing. A small snack could follow; it is important for a foster child to know that the food and the nurturance will continue to be present. The snack should not be too heavy or include caffeinated items that might keep the child awake. After the snack, providing some time for the parent and child to sit and quietly talk or read together or engage in a nurturing though quiet activity continues the pattern of reducing activity, providing a sense of nurturance and support, and preparing a child to fall asleep. After the child uses the bathroom, brushes his teeth, and goes to bed, the rule should be that he stay in bed. He may read, but he may not engage in any active behavior. If he is not tired enough to fall asleep immediately, reading is useful, as it reduces activity, and it also can help the child fall asleep. It also helps to reduce a possible battleground. Finally, reading is a valuable activity for all children since it reinforces good academic skills.

Thus, if he remains awake, the child may choose a behavior that is both relaxing and beneficial at the same time. In time, this type of pattern will positively reinforce her, will lead to improved sleep patterns, and will allow her to sleep through the night, waking up more refreshed than with the irregular bedtime pattern she was used to. As we discussed in Chapter 1, the chaos of abusive and neglectful homes leads to a great deal of insecurity, but such routines reduce the insecurity for the child in foster care.

Similarly, establishing a regular pattern of getting ready for and attending school also helps the foster parents and foster child with school functioning. Many children who come into foster care have had very sporadic school attendance. Many are poor achievers and require assistance in structuring their school activity and attendance. By providing a routine and structure, foster parents enable foster children to improve the likelihood of progressing academically. For example, planning the morning routine so that the child experiences the same activity each morning reduces the child's anxiety and increases his security in school. Waking up at the same time, getting dressed, eating breakfast, and having some relaxing time at the same time every day improves the likelihood that the child will go to school with a healthier attitude.

In school, many foster children require more structure and organization from teachers than other children. Foster parents and teachers can work together to ensure that schoolwork is completed, homework is done, and progress is made. Structuring after-school activities to include playtime, homework time, snack time, TV time, and the like, will go a long way toward providing the child with a more relaxed atmosphere and reducing his anxiety about school performance. Foster parents need to help organize and structure the child's time and activities since the foster child has had so much chaos in his life.

Using Rules to Provide Freedom

Foster parents can also utilize consistent rules to increase feelings of security and to reduce the foster child's anxiety in their home. Essentially, there are two types of rule that parents use with children. One type of rule refers to the tasks that a child is expected to perform, such as making the bed, doing the dishes, and cleaning the room. The other type of rule defines acceptable and unacceptable behaviors, such as "no hitting," "no cursing," saying "thank you," and the like. For both types of rule, there are three criteria that make them effective: they must be clearly stated and well understood by the child, they must be sensible, and they must be enforceable.

For a rule to be clear, all of its parts must be well defined. Rather than simply state that a bedroom should be "clean," it is better to define *clean* for the child, such as by saying, "Clothes picked up, bed made, closet door closed, and no toys on the floor." If the room is cleaned in that way, the job has been done and the rule has been followed. A sensible rule is one that is reasonable and possible for the child to carry out. Setting rules for small tasks is often a good way to begin with foster children. Overloading a new foster child with too many rules, or avoiding rules altogether, is not helpful to the child.

Finally, for a rule to be effective, the foster parents must be willing to enforce it before they issue it. A parent can stipulate that a task must be completed before the child can participate in an important or pleasurable activity. For example, telling Johnny that he must "clean" (well defined) his room before he plays is easier to enforce and less stressful than continually arguing about when the room will be cleaned. By following the three criteria for good rules, foster parents provide freedom and security in the foster home.

Consistency

A common thread throughout our discussion of structure and rules has been the theme of consistency. Consistency helps to weave a bond of security for the foster child. The parents' behavior should be the same in a given situation, no matter what the circumstances are. For example, dinner is always at the same time, in spite of the fact that certain circumstances may disrupt the schedule. Similarly, the bedtime routine does not change, even if the specific bedtime might sometimes need to change. The child must *always* follow the rule to clean his room before going out to play, and the child must *always* be reprimanded if he hits another child. The closer the parent can get to perfect consistency, the easier it is for the foster child. No parent can be 100 percent consistent; it is impossible to be "perfect." But by being as consistent as possible in many areas, foster parents can go a long way to reducing the foster child's insecurity and helping her improve her adjustment to foster care.

Consistency is important, first, because it enables a child to predict the behavior of his foster parents. He can feel secure in the knowledge that the world is safe, that his impulses will not be overwhelming, and that his "badness" will not cause the foster parents to disintegrate or to act as his own parents did toward him. By testing rules and limits, children begin to understand the limits of their own autonomy, get a sense of social responsibility, and feel more secure regarding their own impulses. Foster parent consistency provides the stability that helps the child with these important psychological tasks.

While this is important for all children, foster children need a greater degree of consistency from their foster parents because of the amount of chaos that most of them experienced earlier in their lives. It is critical for the development of their ego structures and their socialization skills that foster parents maintain a high degree of consistency. Foster children test the limits of the relationship to the highest possible degree, and unless foster parents can withstand this and remain stable, a situation can easily result in which the foster child feels rejected and/or abused all over again. Rules in the foster home and the rules of society both enable foster parents to remove themselves somewhat from these struggles. Thus, foster parents can remain nurturing and affectionate toward the foster child while being very strict, consistent, and absolute regarding the structures and demands they place upon the foster child.

Foster children often develop the neurotic component to their personality known as "repetition compulsion." Repetition compulsion is the need to repeat experiences that have happened earlier in one's life. The foster child who has previously been abused, neglected, and/or abandoned feels a need to repeat behaviors in the foster home that can verify her "badness." Because of this, foster children test rules and limits more than other children to force the foster parents to reject them once again. If the foster parents *do* reject the foster child (and unfortunately, this sometimes occurs), it reinforces the child's belief in her own badness and makes it that much more difficult for her in her next environment. By taking into account the developmental needs of the child and her special needs in relation to foster care, and by providing rules and structure, foster parents can go a long way to reducing the foster child's insecurity and helping her adjust within the home. By doing all this in a consistent and structured manner, the foster parents are not rejecting; the rules and structure reduce the power struggles and leave the relationship more positive and supportive.

Ethical Considerations

As part of their preparation, foster families must accept certain ethical standards in providing quality care. Foster family care recognizes that the family is *the* special unit that can best nurture children to the fullest mental and emotional development. Although foster care is expected to be temporary, foster families must have commitment, compassion, and faith in the dignity and worth of children, and they must be willing to work with the agency to develop and carry out a plan of care for the child. Each foster parent has an obligation to maintain and improve the practice of fostering and to perform this function with integrity, competence, and compassion. Foster parents must see their primary obligation as the welfare of the child in their care.

Foster parents also need to recognize that the foster child may be reluctant to discuss his past. Opening up about this very private part of his life may be unsettling to him. It is the child, not the foster parents, who must determine whether the past is talked about and the way it is talked about if it is. Oftentimes, social service workers shield foster parents from part of the past because of the child's right to confidentiality. The foster parents also have an obligation to keep confidential from the community all information pertaining to foster children placed in their home. This is to ensure the rights of the foster child.

It is important for foster parents to use appropriate channels for developing and refining their own skills. Ongoing education and foster parent training are essential parts of this process. Participation in foster parent associations and working closely with social service agencies is in the best interests of the foster child. Essentially, the foster parents are responsible for the quality and extent of care they provide.

Foster parents need to be open to the values expressed by the foster child. Clearly, foster care needs to be approached without discrimination by sex, race, or culture, even though foster children may have negative or stereotypical feelings about a certain race or religion. Most children imitate or model their parents' values, and foster children too may come into care with a variety of prejudices. Foster families with an air of acceptance can begin to provide appropriate values to the foster child that are more compatible with the values of society in general. By initially accepting and potentially redirecting the child's values, foster families play an important role in the child's moral development. Helping foster children learn right from wrong and encouraging positive moral standards is part of the ethics involved in foster parenting.

Finally, foster parents must respect the role that the biological parents play in the child's life. It is important not to criticize or denigrate the biological parents but to simply listen and provide support to the foster child at times of frustration. The child may regard behavior that probes the past as derogatory of the biological parents, which can lead to strained relationships in the foster family. By supporting the role of the biological parents, helping the child to sort out his emotions associated with them, and maintaining a neutral position in relation to the biological parents, the foster family can help the child with his emotional growth and development.

Preparing the Family and the Community for the Foster Child

The foster family, more than any other part of the foster care system, has the potential to make the greatest impact on the child's growth and development, but the child also has an impact on the family that she enters. Inclusion of a foster child automatically alters the family system that existed prior to her placement. Families are most successful when they are kept in balance, when interactions between parents and children are generally positive, and when everyone generally knows his place within the system. When this gets disrupted or changed with the addition of the foster child, the roles of all the family members are shifted. Relationships become altered, and frequently day-to-day activities become disrupted.

Knowing this in advance and preparing the family for the foster child can help prevent problems. Before placement, the foster family needs to address existing roles in the family's day-to-day life—in particular, those of the children in the family—to help understand what the "new" family system will be like. Moreover, the marriage and the kinds of changes that can be anticipated in it should be discussed in advance. Couples who are expecting the birth or adoption of a child commonly do this, but it is often neglected before the arrival of a foster child. Parents and children need to recognize that a foster child will bring his own personal habits, expectations, and behaviors to the family system. While families generally understand the demands and expectations a newborn infant will bring, it is more difficult to imagine the demands that a new, older child might bring to the foster home. Brainstorming, values clarification, sharing concerns, and other similar activities help prepare the family for the kinds of changes that may be anticipated.

Not only should major issues such as space, sharing, and how to get along be looked at, but so should such seemingly minor issues as meals, favorite foods, television time, and favorite TV shows. If the family is prepared for the child's habits, behaviors, and fears, everyone's anxiety can be reduced. Thus, it is important for the foster family to have an advance sense of the prospective child's day-to-day habits, preferences, and interests. Hopefully, the social worker can provide this information prior to placement. But even without this information, if the family members have shared common concerns, the family system can be more prepared for the arrival of the foster child.

Another way the family system can prepare itself for the foster child is to recognize the effects that the child may have upon the family. Couples can recall ways their relationship changed with addition of their biological children. But the behavioral problems of the foster child can unwittingly increase tension and arguments over discipline and child management. The foster child will clearly extract a certain amount of energy and time from the foster parents, and the parents need to understand how the marital relationship will change as a result of foster care placement. If both foster parents are equally committed to fostering, their relationship can weather situational stresses that may occur. Utilizing joint discussions and positive problem-solving skills can help prepare them for the foster child.

The biological children of the foster parents need to adjust as well. Oftentimes, biological children are afraid or frustrated because they may have to share or give up their bedrooms. They may become concerned about community embarrassment, or they may worry that their parents will not have enough time for them. These and any similar issues need to be addressed before placement of a child, if possible. By focusing ahead of time on these issues and recognizing the feelings of their biological children, parents reinforce the positive values and family motives to foster care that will also help prepare the children.

Finally, community and relatives often need to be prepared. Notifying the school, informing doctors, and talking with the minister or rabbi are all community steps that ease the transition into foster care. By sharing their goals and informing their friends and community members, the foster family can help make the transition a more comfortable one for the foster child. The family's close relatives also need to be included in discussions about the prospective fostering to eliminate undue tensions that may get displaced onto the foster child. Not everyone in the family will understand or agree with a family's decision to become a foster family, and discussion and preparation ahead of time will ease the transition and hopefully lead to more positive experiences for both the foster family and the foster child. If the foster family can anticipate sources of resistance, whether from the marriage, from biological children, or from the community or relatives, they can deal with this resistance ahead of time and reduce the concerns. Since foster care is not an isolated family experience, foster families can use outside family and community relationships to positively impact the foster care experience.

The First Day

The day a foster child arrives at the foster home is a unique experience for both family and child. Many concrete behaviors and situations will be encountered in the typical first day in the foster home. The following list is meant for understanding and is not meant to be an exhaustive list of all of the new situations that can develop between a foster child and a foster family. The list, rather, is intended to give a clear understanding of the experience from the eyes of the foster child.

1. Being transported with the social worker to the new home.
2. Feeling tense and nervous along the way.
3. Arriving at the foster home.
4. Meeting the foster family members who are at home.
5. Touring the house and new room.
6. Asking questions of the social worker.
7. Saying good-bye to the social worker.
8. Using the bathroom.
9. Eating meals in the home.
10. Meeting children and others in the home as they come home from school or work.
11. Meeting friends, relatives, and others in the community.

12. Touring the neighborhood.

13. Participating in "family" activities.

14. Getting ready for bed.

15. Trying to settle down the tension.

16. Dealing with special concerns or problems, especially at night (such as bedwetting, nightmares, eating problems, medications).

17. Learning a new bedtime routine.

18. Waking up with the family on the following day.

19. Getting ready for school. Eating breakfast with the foster family.

20. Breathing a sigh of relief at having survived the first twenty-four hours.

Having survived this first day, the family and the child will embark on a journey in which they learn about each other, share their mutual values, ideas, and behaviors, and develop the new, if temporary, family system. If the family has been prepared through discussion and clarification of ideas and emotions, if the foster child feels that she has a *real* place within the family, if the family provides her with a sense of consistency, structure, and support, if they maintain an ethical posture, and if the child and the family are prepared to deal with "anything that comes up," the foster care experience can become a rewarding one for all.

Special problems can develop over the course of foster care, and the next chapter presents a discussion of why they occur, as well as suggests some management techniques to address them. By preparing ahead and knowing what to expect, the foster care experience can be beneficial to the child and rewarding for the overall family system.

3

Overview of Special Needs from a Developmental Perspective

T HE special needs of foster children are very much related to their age. Foster children at different ages have different special needs because of their different stages of psychological growth and development. Age influences the way children adjust to changes in their lives and to foster care in particular, but emotional development and maturity seem to have a greater impact upon the special needs of foster children and upon their adjustment within the foster care setting. Issues of attachment, separation, bonding; feelings of vulnerability and inadequacy; feelings about being in foster care at all; aggressiveness and destructiveness—all are affected by both the emotional and the psychological development of the child. At different psychological ages, these issues play varying roles and have varying impacts on a child's adjustment to foster care. This chapter will focus on these issues, with a special focus on the child's chronological and psychological development.

Attachment–Separation and the Newborn

The most critical psychological issue affecting children coming into foster care is the issue of attachment and separation. For the newborn, this is not a real issue, but through the symbiotic relationship of parent and infant, bonds develop that lead to psychological attachment. When an older child is abruptly removed from that environment and placed into foster care, psychological depression will often result due to this attachment. Abrupt removal of children who have a psychological attachment to the biological parents is generally quite traumatic.

But young foster children who have been removed from their biological parents rarely have had a stable psychological relationship with those parents. Placement is almost always the result of an ongoing family problem or crisis, and the child has probably experienced months, if not years, in a physically and/or emotionally unhealthy environment. Thus, only fragments of a healthy psychological relationship have formed, and a great deal of turmoil remains in the parent-child relationship. Adjustment for young children in foster care is made easier if nurturing foster parents meet the physical needs without placing any unusual demands upon the emotional needs of the child. Often, very young children's developmental growth has been delayed, especially in interactive aspects of development, such as talking, socialization, and toilet training. In young children in particular, the problems that led to foster care most often manifest themselves in a variety of regressive behaviors and in immaturity.

Recently, there has been a significant increase in the number of infants coming into foster care as a result of drug addiction of the parents. Most of these infants are drug-dependent themselves, and they require very special treatment, to be discussed in later chapters. But for infants who come into foster care not yet attached to anyone and without drug dependency, providing a basic warm, nurturing environment that is healthy for infants is usually sufficient for their needs.

The Toddler Years (The "Terrible Twos")

The toddler years are the most difficult years for the foster child. The psychologically healthy child in a healthy home environment moves through a process of separation and individuation that leads to feelings of security, self-worth, and a healthy identity. But foster children have often had a great deal of unevenness in their attachment, and because their relation to this attachment is tentative, they often feel threatened and emotionally vulnerable. They fear separation because of this weak attachment, and when separation occurs and they are placed into foster care, their emotional functioning regresses. These foster children become clingy, dependent, and highly vulnerable.

Such toddlers see the world as a very scary place because to them, it *has* been scary. In the short two or three years of their lives, these foster children have already experienced abuse, chaos, and real separation that makes it very difficult for emotional attachment to form. A toddler may exhibit temper tantrums, destructive behavior, depression, withdrawal, and other symptoms that emerge from these strong feelings of vulnerability and fear of the world around him. The child fears that the relationship with the foster parent, once formed, will be disrupted, and all too often these very young children are moved several times in emergency foster care before finding a more secure placement. Since young foster children have a limited ability to trust, they fear that the foster parent will treat them as their biological parents did, exacerbating their problems.

As such, the toddler-age foster child needs all the physical and emotional nurturance, warmth, stability, and security possible. It is the foster parents' responsibility to understand the reasons for the foster child's behavior and to respond appropriately to his emotional needs. The foster parent needs to recognize that a regression is necessary for healthy and reasonable psychological growth to take place. The foster child who remains detached, aloof, and uninvolved with the foster parents will likely be irreparably damaged in terms of his psychological growth and development.

Unfortunately, a child's emotional growth is at odds with the customary practices of foster care. It is often felt that the foster parents should not encourage attachment because the child is likely to return home. But if the young child does *not* develop an attachment to an adult figure early in life, the child may never overcome the negative effects of not going through the separation-individuation process. Hence, children between two and four years old whose psychological attachment with the biological parent is impaired will usually need to remain in foster care long enough to resolve these issues with the foster parent. For such children, it is *critical* that a stable, nurturing foster family be found, one with whom the child will be able to remain throughout her time in foster care. Further disruptions of foster care for any reason during this time will further impair the child's emotional development. If the foster parents can recognize the emotional needs of these children and respond like parents as soon as possible, the foster children may be able to overcome this trauma during the process of separation and individuation.

The Preschooler and Feelings of Vulnerability and Inadequacy

For children of preschool years, adjustment to foster care is somewhat different. Adjustment continues to be affected by the degree to which the child was able to move through separation and individuation. Once a child has developed a sense of self, separate from others, and has begun to understand that there is good and bad within himself as well as within the parents, adjustment to foster care is much easier. Because of previous chaos and abuse, however, most children who enter foster care have continuing difficulties. Unlike the toddler, who is struggling to develop a sense of self and autonomy, the preschooler has to struggle with feelings of vulnerability and inadequacy in comparison with others. Most foster children of all ages face this, and in fact, vulnerability is the primary psychological effect of abuse, neglect, and placement away from home. Feelings of vulnerability are the *key* psychological effect of abuse and neglect. The child sees herself as "bad" and believes that the reason she has been abused is because of the badness within her. This child believes that she causes trouble wherever she goes, and she fears continual hurt. She often sets up circumstances in foster care that "prove" to herself and to others how "bad" she truly is. When children are abused, they rarely blame the parents and almost always believe that they deserve the parents' abusive behavior.

At the preschool age, many symptoms may reflect these problems. Young children can't verbalize their feelings, and they have a greater tendency to "act out" their feelings in destructive ways. As such, young foster children often have symptoms of poor impulse control, frequent temper tantrums, instability, depression, destructiveness, poor self-esteem, and poor socialization with peers.

Like the toddler, the preschooler often clings and has continued difficulties separating from foster parents. In addition, the preschooler often has difficulty learning to deal with feelings and emotions, a primary emotional task at that age. The child has difficulty dealing with his anger and in fact sees this anger as another example of his "badness." This, like other behaviors, reinforces the belief that he is a bad child and is responsible for the abuse that he has suffered. If foster care enables a child to resolve the problems in attachment, these symptoms will begin to diminish.

The School-Age Child and School Problems

The school-age child faces difficulties in school, not only in learning but also in peer relationships, following rules, and listening to teachers. Feelings of vulnerability and inadequacy surface in a way that affects each of these tasks. Foster children do not believe in themselves, and they tend to isolate themselves from others. In addition, because they are generally afraid of the world around them, the way they maintain their isolation can affect all major tasks of school-age children.

The major task of school-age children is learning. Children who feel anxiety and stress in their lives have more difficulty learning than children who feel free and relaxed. Most studies of children with learning problems show that emotional problems interfere with learning in many ways. For the foster child, who feels vulnerable and inadequate and who lacks self-confidence, learning is a very difficult task. Many foster children are sad and depressed, and they spend a great deal of their school time thinking of their home and family problems. A large number of foster children exhibit hyperactive behavior in the classroom. While hyperactivity is commonly caused by a mild brain dysfunction, it is also sometimes caused by the child's need to defend against his own depression. Another behavioral reaction is withdrawal, in which the foster child appears lethargic, daydreams, and simply does not do the work. Even if the child tries to do schoolwork, his limited self-confidence and poor frustration tolerance may cause significant learning problems.

Another major task for the school-age child is to develop and improve relationships with peers. Children of this age enjoy games, and the rules of these games help their socialization. Both structured activities (school activities, sports, and recreation) and unstructured activities (recess, after-school playground activity, and playing at a friend's house) provide an opportunity for children to learn relationships and have fun. Some foster children do reasonably well in structured activity, but they generally do poorly in unstructured activities. Foster children are often uncomfortable around peers and set themselves up for situations in which peers treat them as their biological parents did. On the playground, these children may start fights or be easily victimized, and such behavior can confirm and reinforce a child's belief that he is bad. Other foster children often feel alienated from others, and they isolate themselves or withdraw, feeling as if they can't fit in. Moreover many foster children do not have the emotional strength to function well without external structure, which may lead to greater problems during recess and in unsupervised playground activity.

Finally, it is often difficult for foster children to deal well with authority figures, such as teachers and principals. Out of anger and fear, they tend to enter relationships with authority figures tentatively, and they often set up situations in which there are problems. If they are afraid, they avoid contact with authority figures, often expecting them to get out of control, just like their abusive parents did. If they are angry, they may be negative or have angry outbursts when confronted with homework. If they feel a mixture of emotions (which is most typical), they may need to test the limits of authority and require structure from the authority figure to reduce their anxiety. In all such instances, their experiences before foster placement affect how they relate to authority figures, peers, and schoolwork.

Adolescence and Issues of Emancipation

Many adolescents in foster care live in a residential treatment facility or group home setting. This is primarily because of their greater behavioral problems, including truancy, stealing, vandalism, and community destructiveness. But many adolescents are also placed in foster homes. Like their younger counterparts, foster adolescents continue to struggle with feelings of vulnerability and inadequacy, but they must also deal with the typical adolescent issues of identity formation and a separation of self from parents, to believe that they are capable of functioning on their own. It is the combination of these factors that creates problems typical of the adolescent in foster care.

Like the school-age foster child, the foster adolescent often struggles with authority figures to a much greater extent than is normal. Since many foster adolescents have had chaotic relationships since early in life, they must attempt to resolve problems that they have had since the "terrible twos." This often requires foster parents to exercise rather rigid structures and rules to help. Within the framework of this structure, the parents of foster adolescents may need to allow a high degree of freedom and flexibility to them so that they can resolve these struggles.

For example, the foster parents may set a rule that homework is to be done every night by ten o'clock. That is the "rigid rule." It is important for the parents to let the adolescent determine when to do homework during after-school hours, providing guidance and support. Similarly, a foster adolescent may receive a ten-dollar allowance every week, and the foster parents may provide no further money for entertainment. But the foster adolescent needs to have final determination on how that money is to be spent. This freedom, within the framework of a solid structure, allows the foster adolescent the opportunity to define his own autonomy and identity, while still responding to the rules of the foster parents.

Foster parents should also assist their adolescent foster children with another major task of adolescent development, the development of life goals. Career planning, relationships, trust, and a sense of belonging are all significant issues for the adolescent foster child. Young adolescents also need assistance in planning their schooling. Working with and understanding the adolescent's interest in going to college or in learning a trade can help in planning direction in school. If the adolescent is unsure of his direction, parents may encourage the school to provide some vocational interest testing. By showing an interest in the adolescent's long-range planning, parents can helping him feel that he belongs and that they care about him.

Foster parents may also help the adolescent with the task of identifying those skills that are necessary as she moves toward independent living. Thinking about past and present relationships, issues of self-concept and self-confidence, and assessing skills learned and skills needed are critical steps for the adolescent to take. Foster parents need to recognize that a history of abuse and neglect will probably affect the child's ability to develop these skills, and they will work with her more slowly while she struggles to find *her own* place in the world.

Most adolescents try to balance the demands of school, peer relationships, and jobs, and they need assistance from their parents in doing this. They need to learn how to maintain a checking account, how to find roommates and affordable housing, and how to drive. All these skills give them a greater degree of independence. By paying attention to this and helping the foster adolescent learn new skills, manage money, and balance the many demands in their lives, foster parents can significantly assist them in a way that also promotes trust and develops a sense of belonging within the family.

Finally, foster adolescents approaching the age of eighteen are often at a serious disadvantage. They continue to feel torn between their foster parents and their biological parents, and they don't know who to call their family. They are likely to turn to both families for advice and will feel loyalty conflicts if the advice they receive is conflicting. Because they often remain insecure and feel that they don't quite fit in anywhere, many foster adolescents fear their impending emancipation and show obvious signs of this in their behavior. These adolescents need to be listened to and supported, and they should be given every opportunity to develop their own plans for the future. While foster parents may feel that the adolescent is making mistakes, and they may want to provide guidance and advice, it is critical for the foster adolescent and his developing identity to know that he can decide his own direction for the future. By providing reassurance about belonging to the foster family and showing a desire to continue the relationship after the adolescent reaches "adulthood," foster parents can help reduce this insecurity and anxiety and smooth the way toward emancipation. Many adult foster children maintain relationships with their foster parents, which proves to be quite rewarding both to the adult child and to his former foster parents.

This chapter has outlined the varying developmental needs of children who come into foster care. While common issues exist among foster children of all ages, such as feelings of vulnerability and inadequacy, depression, fear, and insecurity, these emotions manifest themselves in very different ways depending on the chronological and psychological age of the child. By understanding this, the foster parent can provide the critical help the child needs to continue her psychological and emotional development. The reader should keep this in mind through the following chapters, which address more specific emotions and behaviors that are often problematic for foster children.

4

Emotional Impact
of Placement on
the Foster Child

As we have seen, the primary psychological effect of abuse and neglect and removal from the biological parents' home is a feeling of psychological vulnerability. This vulnerability, which reflects the child's feelings of insecurity and inadequacy in relation to the world around him, affects every aspect of his behavior while in care. Many foster children see the world as a scary place, a place that not only does not nurture but also hurts. Obviously, foster care seeks to reduce these feelings and help the children feel more secure and adequate in comparison with others.

But numerous other feelings, while they are experienced to some degree by all children, are worsened by placement in foster care. These feelings include—but are not limited to—loss, grief, depression, shock, anger, despair, confusion, ambivalence, fantasy, alienation, rejection, dependency, and other feelings. This chapter will focus on these "negative" feelings and their impact upon the foster child. Not all children experience all these feelings, and there is no way to determine ahead of time the extent to which a child will experience various feelings. The key to helping the foster child with these feelings is to accept them, to help her understand them, and to learn appropriate behavioral responses to the emotion.

Grief

Because separation is an inherent part of the foster care process, some pain obviously takes place. Separation is never painless, even for the child who is detached from or has a poor attachment to the biological parents. Separation from the family is traumatic for the child and is necessary only when it is decided that separation is less damaging than remaining in the biological home. If foster parents are aware that separation is inherently painful for the child, they can help the foster child with the process of dealing with the pain and the "grief" the child feels.

Most children who experience a significant loss, such as the move of a close friend, the death of a grandparent, or an illness, have a solid emotional base that assists and promotes their healing after the loss. In the foster child, however, this emotional foundation is often impaired. But the foster child must still deal with this grief. She will typically experience four basic steps until the grief has been adequately resolved: shock, anger, despair, and acceptance.

The initial response to grief is shock, and with it comes denial, or a blocking of any emotions associated with the grief. Early on, the foster child appears rather numb to the foster care experience. It is almost as if she has no feelings. Sometimes foster children even act happy during the early stages of their grief. A "honeymoon" period is very common during foster care. During the honeymoon period, foster children behave almost perfectly. But they are very much afraid of doing anything wrong, and they relate in a fairly superficial manner and remain numb to all their feelings. This is primarily because of the shock of their removal from their family and their gradual need to experience the feelings that have been generated by placement with another family. Obviously, during the early stages of placement, foster parents need to provide a great deal of structure and nurturance to help the child get used to the family's habits and routines.

The second stage of grief is anger at having been placed in foster care. Typically during this stage, the anger is outwardly directed and may involve behavior such as rebelliousness, negativism, and destructiveness. The child may even run away, hoping to "find" the biological parents again. Feelings of rejection and abandonment may surface, and the subsequent anger is often directed at the abusing parents. As the anger grows, so does a general feeling of upset, with frequent temper tantrums and similar outward signs of anger. Anger is often the most difficult emotion for foster parents to deal with, especially if the foster parents do not understand why the child feels and acts angry.

All too often, when foster children begin expressing their anger, they are moved to a new home. This is highly unfortunate, however, as it reinforces the child's sense of "badness" and creates a pattern in which she is afraid to understand and express her emotions. It is critical for foster children to have sensitive and understanding foster parents who can realize the necessity of helping the child deal with her anger. By showing strength and patience, by providing structure and support, the foster child can begin to reduce her angry behavior and adjust to foster care.

The third stage of grief is a period of despair. During this stage, the child's feelings are directed inward more than outward, perhaps because he has exhausted his energy while acting out the angry feelings. Despair also occurs because the child realizes that he has been removed from his home and that despite all efforts, he remains in foster care. His despair is the result of the realization that he will not return to the biological family in the foreseeable future. After this realization takes place, he becomes more depressed, feels both more helpless and more hopeless, and tends to become more withdrawn and apathetic. At school, peer relationships may improve, but simultaneously academic work may deteriorate. During this period of time, the child needs to fully understand the facts related to his foster placement, but he should also begin to talk about his feelings, especially acknowledging the sadness and hopelessness that he feels. Essentially, these feelings of despair, depression, hopelessness, and isolation need to be treated sympathetically, so that the child knows that he is accepted even though he is experiencing and expressing such feelings.

During the final stage of grief, acceptance, the child begins to accept the fact of having been placed in foster care and to function more appropriately within the foster family and community. She may even develop a detachment from her abusing family, a detachment that enables her to function better in the foster family. More stability occurs, and overall emotional development improves. During this time, the child continues to think about the biological family and may talk more about them and her good and bad memories. Obviously, when children talk about these memories, they need to be supported, and foster parents and therapists need to refrain from taking a position that the biological parents are "bad." It is extremely helpful for the child to be able to express his feelings and for him to understand that he has a right to his feelings. If the foster parents are not careful, though, they can complicate things by accepting as fact that the biological parents are "bad" and by telling this to the child. By listening, supporting, and nurturing the child's feelings, while providing appropriate parenting, foster parents can help the child in this final stage of the grief process.

Confusion

Another common emotion foster children feel is confusion. The foster child rarely understands the details and circumstances that led to her placement, no matter what she has been told by social workers or other adults. Part of the reason for this is that she is often given conflicting messages, since biological parents, social workers, and foster parents may tell her different things about why she is in care. At the same time, even if the child is told the "truth" about her placement, her ability to understand and deal with its ramifications may be somewhat limited. All this leads to the confusion a foster child feels as she enters foster care. It is important for the foster parents to provide factual information to the child, in conjunction with the social worker, which will hopefully reduce the confusion, and it is helpful to encourage the foster child to express her beliefs and ideas in order to clarify them. Most important, if the child understands the reasons for her placement, the source of the confusion can be reduced.

In addition, foster children are often confused by rules, events, and circumstances in the new family, school, and community. For children who have had sporadic school attendance, it is confusing to go to school on a daily basis. For children who have been abused, it is often confusing when someone acts pleasantly and nicely to them, especially if the child believes that he is "bad" and deserves negative attention. In the foster home, the child will generally have many new experiences that are confusing to him simply because the style of his new life is so different. Until he gets accustomed to his new environment and stays in it long enough to experience some pleasant and consistent relationships, his confusion will likely surface in many ways. As usual, the more predictable a foster family is and the more the child can rely on the family's consistency, the more easily he will overcome these feelings of confusion in the foster home.

Anger

Anger has a relationship to grief, associated with placement away from home, but there are many other sources of anger for the foster child. These sources of anger are generally related to the way the child was treated—in particular, to the physical or emotional abuse that the child has suffered. The child may also feel anger at society and at the adults in general who allowed this abuse to take place or who removed him from his family. Finally, many foster children's anger is directed toward the self because the child believes that he is "bad." In fact, it is the self-directed anger that is often the most damaging to the child, as it contributes greatly to the depression that many foster children experience.

To help the child with his anger, both the foster parents and the child first must recognize that it is all right to be angry, and that angry behavior can be understood as well as redirected. Clearly, there should be concise and rigid rules about inappropriate expressions of anger, such as destructiveness or physical assaultiveness. But the foster child also needs to know the appropriate and acceptable ways in which he can express anger. Certainly, verbal expressions of anger and talking about angry feelings must be acceptable, but it may also help to provide physical outlets, through athletics, punching bags, drawing, or other activities. These are all positive ways to assist the child to more adequately express his anger. Foster children need to know that any verbal expression of anger is accepted as long as the anger is understood. Foster parents need to recognize that the child's anger may be directed at a variety of different objects, including the child himself, the foster family, peers, and teachers. The anger is generally associated with the abuse or neglect that he has suffered, but it may also be associated with the feelings of rejection and abandonment that foster children almost universally feel.

Alienation, Withdrawal, and Isolation

Foster children often feel alienated from everyone and very alone, as if they do not belong. In normal development, children learn to belong to a group by being part of a family. But when a foster child is placed in foster care, a sense of isolation and alienation arises. Therapists hear numerous expressions of these feelings in large part because foster children do not believe they fit in anywhere. Foster children "really" aren't part of a family, so they don't fit in there. They don't fit in at school because they may attend the school for only a short period of time. When children come into a foster home, it is often difficult for them to make new friends, and many foster children do not participate in typical children's activities, such as neighborhood sports, birthday parties, and sleepovers. Their response to these feelings of alienation is to withdraw and become isolated, and foster children sometimes have difficulty making new friends or feeling any sense of attachment within the foster family because of their alienation. Foster children may not wish to cause trouble (many believe that they cause trouble wherever they go), and one way of avoiding this is to remain isolated. Thus, between feelings of abandonment and alienation, they avoid relationships and choose to remain alone.

It is very important for foster parents to subtly encourage active participation with others. If the alienated child can be encouraged to feel part of a group, whether a peer group, a family group, or some other social group, it can help reduce feelings of alienation, as well as some of the negative effects of the feelings of rejection and abandonment. In addition, if foster parents can help children reduce their feelings of isolation and withdrawal, they can learn to overcome some of their negative emotions and can learn that the world is a more nurturing, caring place than it was in their biological home.

Ambivalence

Ambivalence means mixed and opposite feelings, such as rejection and attachment, love and hate, and trust and mistrust. It is very common for foster children to feel much ambivalence. They may be happy to be in foster care and yet angry to be away from their biological family. They love their biological parents, but they are angry at them for how they were treated. They feel warmth and nurturance from the foster parents, but they must remain distant and somewhat isolated within the foster family.

It is critical for foster parents to recognize these feelings of ambivalence, in order to help the child with them. In addition, as the child begins to feel more positively toward her foster parents or more negatively toward her biological parents, she often experiences feelings of guilt, believing that it is "bad" to have such feelings. If foster parents recognize that ambivalence exists and that the foster child is likely to feel guilty, they can help the child understand these feelings and express them in more positive ways.

Relief/Safety and the Need to Test Rules

Many foster children feel a great sense of relief and safety once they are no longer being abused. In their biological home, they were scared and felt quite insecure because of the way they were treated. When they came into the foster home and learned that they would be safe and would be treated differently, they felt a sense of relief. But now they need to test new rules and limits in order to maintain that new safety. Thus, while the child initially feels a sense of relief in foster care, it is only after he tests the rules in his new home and tests the limits of the relationship that he truly feels safe in the world around him. By using the principles of structure and consistency outlined in Chapter 2, foster parents can help the child continue to feel safe and secure in his new environment and within himself.

Dependency and Passivity

Many foster children's physical and emotional needs were neglected by their parents, which leads to negative and angry feelings. They may fear that they will once again not be taken care of, and withdraw and become more passive toward the world around them. In addition, they may remain dependent since their early dependency needs for nurturance and love were never met. This combination is detrimental to their emotional development: they maintain strong feelings of dependency, yet simultaneously become passive toward others. Thus, they wish for their needs to be met, but they stay passive and unable to express those needs. They may fantasize that someone will take care of them without actually taking the steps necessary to make the appropriate changes in their life. If such children do not learn to recognize and express their needs, they may develop a lifelong pattern of inadequate expression of their needs in relationships.

Foster parents can help them by providing the nurturing and care that they need, and by helping them learn to express their needs. Foster children need to know it is both okay and necessary to ask for things and that they are not an imposition on the foster family. By encouraging foster children to express themselves, foster parents can reduce their passivity, while simultaneously helping to meet their needs. The more a child feels accepted in this way, the more she can become assertive and seek appropriate avenues for meeting her needs.

Wishful and Magical Thinking

Because of their problems in the early development of trust, foster children develop a pattern of wishful thinking. Moreover, they may think that their wishful thinking alone is causing things to occur. Many foster children wish bad thoughts, then fear that these very wishes will cause their bad thoughts to come true. Some foster children attempt to avoid reality by pretending that in the biological home things were not as bad as they really were. They may also pretend that they are going home sooner than they really might. Sometimes, foster children wish harm to their abusing parents because of their hurt and anger, and when something does happen, they feel guilty because of those wishes.

These fantasies, wishes, and other thoughts generally play a big role in the emotions that the foster children feel. Foster parents may not be able to elicit the foster child's wishes very easily, but if the foster parents can recognize that all of this exists, they may have a clue when problems develop in foster care. Through the use of therapy, foster children can begin to develop and understand new ways to express their wishes and to face reality in a more appropriate manner. In addition, therapy often brings a reduction in magical thinking and an awareness that one's wishes alone cannot make something occur. This awareness also assists them in overcoming problems of dependency, passivity, alienation, isolation, and confusion. Thus, the beliefs that foster children have, combined with their emotions, create many of their difficulties.

Limited Self-Confidence—Poor Ego Skills

Most foster children's ability to understand what is going on around them is quite limited, and as a result, they have only limited psychological resources. Their ability to deal with frustration, to make friends and play well, to assert their needs, to take risks, to learn in school, and to handle emotions is more limited because of their experiences before coming into foster care. The abuse or neglect, followed by removal from home, create a poor self-image that is very hard to turn around.

This shows up in many forms in the child's behavior. The child may have frequent temper tantrums, lose patience easily, get into fights at school and on the playground, appear depressed, and seem to "need to please." This need to please is less easily understood than the other, more obvious behaviors. Because of the abuse/neglect and/or self-blame, the foster child will sometimes attempt to "be nice" at all costs. One also sees this phenomenon in children of alcoholics, who try to avoid the rages and outbursts of their parents. Because of their fragile egos and limited self-confidence, foster children are afraid of asserting themselves in any way that could lead to further victimization. Yet the effects of this behavior are actually the opposite of what they intend, for such children lose their own sense of self and become nonassertive and follow others, which risks further victimization, continuing a cycle of this pattern.

The best way to help children who appear to lose themselves in their effort to please others at all costs is to help them learn that it is all right for them to think and want for themselves. By helping a child understand his inner feelings, to stop and think before following others, and to assert his rights, foster parents can help him avoid this cycle of behavior. Before the child is capable of this himself, it is often important for the adults to assert those rights on his behalf, as they encourage him to assert his rights for himself. In some ways, therapists take on this task when they listen to children's feelings, help them understand themselves, and speak for them until they are able to speak for themselves.

Finally, a child with very limited self-confidence is often afraid to try to succeed at school. She is afraid to risk failure, and she assumes that she will fail. Many such children simply sit quietly at school, afraid of opening themselves up to the process of learning.

The adults in their lives must encourage learning, while simultaneously nurturing a sense of the possibility of success. They must help the child know and *feel* that it is all right to make mistakes, that it is a natural part of our humanness. By providing support and encouragement, foster parents can hopefully help the child gain enough self-confidence that she can risk failure and learn to try to get along in and learn from the world around her.

In a general way, this chapter has dealt with many of the emotional issues that foster children experience before and during their care. Understanding the initial stages of grief and the fact that placement is never painless can help foster parents understand the early feelings that the foster child experiences. In addition, by knowing many of the other feelings common to foster children, such as confusion, anger, alienation, ambivalence, relief, dependency, passivity, wishful thinking, and poor self-confidence, foster parents can better understand the foster child's emotional needs and how they can assist the child in meeting these needs. Foster parents are not therapists, nor are they trained to be. But by listening, providing a sense of understanding, and seeking therapeutic assistance for their foster children when necessary, they can make the foster care experience a very rewarding one for foster children and can aid in the appropriate development of their emotional growth.

5

Dealing with
Special Problems

W HILE all children encounter problems as they go through the variety of stages of their upbringing, foster children seem to bring special problems to their foster parents. Over the years, I have found that a number of behaviors quite typical of foster children seem to be the most problematic for foster parents. Many foster parents can handle the usual stages that children go through, and the more typical behavior problems such as mild aggressiveness in school, social isolation, mild depression, and minor complaining. Such problems are typical of many children, and foster parents are not very threatened by them. They seem to have a general sense of how to cope with these problems and are willing to work with foster children to help overcome them.

But other behaviors are much more threatening to foster parents and create a sense of being overwhelmed. It is these behaviors that most frequently lead to the removal of a foster child from the foster home. In general, this chapter will treat each of these behaviors in three ways. First, the behavior and typical ways in which it manifests itself in the foster home will be described. There will follow a clinical description of why foster children engage in that behavior. Finally, ways of dealing with the behavior in the most productive manner for parent and child together will be discussed. Many behaviors are best dealt with by using the structures and rules mentioned in Chapter 2. This chapter will provide specific ways to implement those structures and rules.

Lying

The term *lying* is commonly thought of as simply meaning not telling the truth. But lying is not always quite as simple as that. Lying can mean telling half-truths, omitting portions of the truth that are critical to understanding, or simply fabricating a story that has no basis in reality. The range of possible behaviors in lying is quite large, and certain kinds of lies are often socially acceptable, such as the "white lie," in which someone tells a mild untruth to spare someone's feelings. But most parents react strongly and negatively to all forms of lying that they see in their children. Parents often consider that foster children have lied, but they have not yet developed an understanding of the child's history that allows them to distinguish whether the child is lying. In circumstances that are unclear, foster parents often assume a foster child is lying because they do not know the child well enough to assume otherwise. Many foster children are presumed guilty of lying on the basis of minimal evidence simply because a lengthy history of a relationship is yet to be unfolded.

Children lie for a variety of reasons. The most common reason they lie is to avoid a punishment. Many children believe that if they lie about a misdeed and the parent does not recognize the lie, they can avoid a punishment and "skate through" without any pain. To help children learn to stop lying, parents typically punish the lie as well as the misdeed—in essence, doubling the punishment. They hope that the lying will stop once the child recognizes that it is more detrimental than the truth.

But foster children lie for a variety of other reasons as well. One reason is that foster children have a tendency to tune out the world around them. They pay less attention because the world has been chaotic and negative toward them. As a result, they are often unaware of details that others see, and hence say things in good faith that are later found to be untrue. This type of lie is most typically a half-truth in which the child honestly believes that she is telling the truth, in spite of the parents' belief that she has lied. Until children can begin to approach the world in a more open manner and perceive events around them as others do, it is difficult to control this kind of lying.

One example of this is a child who comes home from school saying that he has no homework, when the foster parent knows that an assignment was given out. The foster child truly believes that no homework was assigned simply because he has not paid attention in the classroom. Thus, the child has not really lied, but the foster parent, not knowing that the child "tunes out" the world around him, believes he has lied in order to avoid the work. In such instances, it is probably best to avoid a power struggle about "truth," but the foster parents need to tell the child that there *is* homework and to encourage the child to find a way to get the assignment (by calling friends or phoning the teacher). In this way, the child can do the assignment, and the family avoids a power struggle around whether a lie took place. In other words, it is typically best to avoid conflicts around lies that occur as a result of reduced perception by the child, and to simply get the job done.

More severe cases of lying may result from a greater degree of disturbance within the foster child, so that the child has a distorted sense of reality that shows up in certain situations. Rather than being limited, the child's perception is distorted. For example, a child who has been seriously abused, accompanied by a lot of yelling and screaming, might perceive that a foster parent is trying to hurt him whenever a foster parent yells at him. The foster parent may view this as a lie, but it is really related to the child's distorted sense of reality, based on his perception that yelling and abuse were often simultaneous behaviors in the past. Again, rather than getting into conflicts about whether a lie took place, in such situations it is better for the foster parent to calmly present the reality of the situation. He should simply and calmly tell the child that all he did was yell, and he should remind the child that he has not been abused, even if he feels that he was about to be. Again, by avoiding a conflict about the possible lie, the foster parent can help the child with her distorted sense of reality and reduce the insecurity associated with her earlier life.

Another severe form of lying common among foster children is telling the blatant story that never really happened. The child is aware of the fact that his blatant story is made up, but he tells it as if it were true. For example, a child might tell his social worker that his foster parents have abused him, which sets in motion a series of events, including an investigation of possible abuse and anger on the part of the foster parents. But the child knows that the abuse did not take place. He said so simply in order to create chaos, perhaps unconsciously trying to achieve a chaotic experience like his earlier experiences, to confirm how "bad" he is.

In addition, the foster child gets a great deal of attention as a result of a blatant lie, whether positive or negative. Foster children often have strong needs for attention, and a child might lie in order to get the attention she believes she cannot get in any other way. Such attention actually reinforces lying rather than punishing it. Other examples of fabrications might be the child who says that she is doing great in school, although she is really doing poorly. A child may try to cover up feelings of inadequacy or inferiority by presenting himself as more omnipotent, capable, and successful than he truly is. In such instances, the blatant lie helps the child alter his self-image, as opposed to tuning out or distorting reality. These foster children are aware of the fact that they are lying, but they need to do so in order to feel worse or better about themselves.

The best way to deal with the blatant lie is to confront it directly. It is important for the foster parents to point out that the statements are not true, but they should do so in a way that tells the foster child that they recognize that there are probable reasons why he is lying. Rather than allow the child to get into a power struggle about the lie, it is best not to ask the child if he has lied but simply to point out the reality. Rather than ask, "Why did you lie?" it is simply better if the foster parent says something like, "I know that sometimes you feel like lying because it makes you feel better [or worse], but that is not a reason to lie in this family." Then the foster parent can get into a discussion about alternative behaviors that might bring the child the attention she wants, and that can also help her recognize the feelings associated with her behavior. In this way, the foster parent can reduce the tension around the lying itself and can recognize that the child is not doing it just to be angry or mean or to hurt the foster parent, and together they can work on trying to find other behaviors that are more acceptable to the foster parent.

A final reason why some foster children lie is that they have not learned that it is unacceptable. Again, most foster children have had very chaotic backgrounds, and many have been taught to lie by their abusing parents or have been lied to a great deal of their life. In modeling this behavior, these children lie because they see nothing wrong with it and because they believe it will get them something they want. For example, teenagers may say they have gone to school when they have actually truanted, or younger children may say that a friend gave them a particular toy when they actually stole it from a store. These children are lying not because of a distorted sense of reality and not to reinforce a sense of badness or to counter a sense of inadequacy, but because they believe it is the best thing to do in that situation. Such children show little or no remorse when they lie because it is internalized as an acceptable behavior.

This type of lying is often the most difficult for foster parents to cope with because they would like to see at least a little remorse in the child. Knowing this, a child who lies under these circumstances may even show mild remorse in order to manipulate the foster parent into believing that he feels remorse when he really feels none.

Nonetheless, it is very important for the foster parents to point out the reality and not to question why or whether a lie took place. But it is also important to provide some type of meaningful punishment in order to reinforce that lying is not acceptable behavior. The child who takes something that does not belong to him, must not only return the item, but possibly give up an item that he enjoys using for a week. The adolescent who lies about school must not only be given a structure in which she cannot truant without the parent knowing about it, but her time in which to play until her school behavior and attendance improves could be reduced. By reinforcing the "fact" that lying is not acceptable and by making it one of the rules of the house, it may be possible to reduce this type of lying. But it is important to recognize that it can be very difficult to do so, especially for older children. By preventing the lie from becoming an issue in the power struggle, foster parents can deal with the behaviors associated with the lie and not get into battling about the lying itself. Finally, if foster parents recognize that the child's lies are not aimed directly at themselves but are an aspect of the child's personality, it is easier for them to use behavioral techniques that can reduce the benefits the foster child can gain from lying.

Stealing

Stealing, in the usual sense, is taking something that does not belong to you. When a child takes another child's toys or money or steals something from a store, the stealing is obvious. But in foster care, a whole variety of behaviors are often considered stealing, though it is hard to understand why foster parents view them as such. The most common example is a foster child accused of stealing food. The foster parents may not have allowed the child all the food he wants to eat. They may have restricted the kind of things or the times or amounts a child can eat. Such limitations set up situations in which children take food for a variety of reasons and thus are potential "stealers" of food.

A slight variation of this "stealing" is the foster child who hoards food, taking it to her room and possibly storing it under her bed or elsewhere. If the parents discover this cache, they accuse the child of stealing the food because she hoarded it rather than ate it. It is unfortunate that many foster parents view this as stealing, and if children have relatively unrestricted access to food, they feel that they belong in the family and the hoarding will diminish.

Other foster children perceive their behavior as "borrowing," especially when it involves taking a foster sibling's toys and hoarding them or keeping them temporarily. In such instances of less than clear-cut stealing, the foster child takes or hoards the items as a result of emotional factors. In typical stealing behaviors, emotional factors are often a major contributor.

The primary emotional reason why children steal is to get materially what they have been unable to receive emotionally. In other words, by taking food (the best example), the foster child symbolically takes the emotional nurturance that he has never received in his life. Having received insufficient love and food, the foster child takes what she has always needed and feels as if she were loved by the foster parent. The material object takes on a symbolic meaning and provides her with a sense of emotional security, well-being, or nurturance. Foster children who steal for this reason often have emotional difficulties such as depression, passive-dependence, and/or oppositional tendencies. Not only do they feel that they have not received the love they need (and usually they are right), they lack the assertive ability and the self-confidence to meet their needs in any way other than stealing.

It is important for foster parents to exclude food from the realm of objects whose taking is considered stealing. One way to help a child feel secure and loved in a foster home is to provide an unlimited supply of food. The giving of food can be structured and the hoarding of food can be discouraged, but it is important to recognize that food is used symbolically as love. Providing an essentially unlimited supply of food will help the foster child feel he that he has an unlimited supply of love in the home. The foster child can learn, too, that just as he cannot be hugged for twenty-four hours a day and *actually* receive affection in an unlimited supply, he also cannot receive food in an unlimited supply, and he can learn to accept it. Nonetheless, to feel accepted, the foster child must be able to see the supply of food as essentially unlimited.

The stealing of other objects is also related to emotional issues, and their emotional sources are much like the emotional sources of lying. The parents' response should not be, first, to ask if or why the child stole something. Rather, the parents should tell the child that they know she has stolen something and that this is unacceptable. It is important that she return the object as soon as possible to the owner in order to reduce the positive reinforcement that she gets if she keeps the object. By avoiding a conflict about stealing, the parent and child can avoid all the reinforcement that she might get for stealing, and they can get to the task of returning the object. But it is also important to remember the emotional relationship between the need for attention and nurturance on the one hand and the stealing on the other. It helps to say something to the child such as "I know that when you feel you haven't gotten very much, you think that you have to take things from people," and then remind the child that she can be nurtured and meet some of her needs in ways other than stealing. The foster parents can encourage her to come to them for positive attention and to tell them that she wants to feel loved to replace the stealing. Helping the child recognize that she is stealing because of her emotional needs will facilitate a process that may end the stealing behavior in time. This type of response is most useful when "stealing" behavior is directly related to emotional needs and to feelings of inadequacy, poor self-image, depression, and passive-dependent behavior.

Another form of "stealing" is clearly related to a lack of conscience and a nonrecognition of social rules. In chaotic families, especially those with a heavy usage of drugs, some children are encouraged to steal or observe that stealing is appropriate behavior. To such children, stealing seems to lack the emotional component indicated above, and they rarely have any remorse for the stealing, except a false remorse that is manipulative. For these children, ways must be found to reduce the opportunity for stealing. Rules that reinforce nonstealing behavior can help, and immediate punishment for stealing and demanding the return of the stolen item are necessary. If the stolen objects are of sufficient value, the police should be involved as a further reinforcement of the social laws against stealing. Oftentimes, the foster parent has no choice but to involve the police, and oftentimes foster children with significant stealing behavior, especially those without an emotional component or remorse, will require placement in some type of group home that has a more disciplined environment.

Regressive Behavior

One way foster children cope with their anxieties and control their impulses about separation from home and relationships is to develop and maintain psychological defenses. Basically, a psychological defense is unconsciously developed by the child to reduce his anxiety, control his impulses, and help him feel more comfortable. The defenses that are most common among foster children are avoidance and denial of feelings, and regression. The avoidance and denial of feelings often leads to problems in stealing, lying, and aggressiveness. Regression, by contrast, is essentially a defense in which the child uses infantile behaviors to control his anxiety or impulses.

There are numerous examples of regressive behavior in children. An eight-year-old who sucks his thumb is engaged in regressive behavior. A five-year-old who has been toilet trained but begins bedwetting or daytime wetting in foster care is exhibiting regressive behavior. Other regressive behaviors can include clinging, masturbating, soiling one's pants, and any other behavior that may be typical for younger children but is considered atypical for a foster child because of his age. In other words, it is not regression when a three-and-a-half-year-old has occasional daytime wetting accidents, because this is age-appropriate behavior, but if a toilet-trained five-year-old soils his pants, that is a form of regression.

The major reason for regressive behavior is to reduce anxiety. Anxiety surfaces because the child cannot deal emotionally with the realities in her life. For example, a child may feel ambivalence toward her birth-mother, missing her yet also being very angry at her because of feelings of rejection or abandonment. She will feel anxiety because she cannot tolerate the ambivalence of loving her mother and being angry at her at the same time. Another foster child may be so angry at his mother because she abandoned him that he sometimes wishes to destroy her. When such children feel that they cannot safely control their impulses, their anxiety will be higher; they fear that they might lose control and destroy someone. A six-year-old child who has witnessed a great deal of sexual and violent behavior and who cannot adequately repress his sexual or aggressive impulses will feel anxious simply because this is so overwhelming emotionally. All these are examples of the kinds of anxiety that can lead to regressive behavior. The child who feels ambivalent, but whose feelings only surface at night in his dreams, might wet the bed. The child who needs to control her impulses may start thumb-sucking to feel more secure and ward off the temptation to harm someone. The child who cannot tolerate his sexual and aggressive impulses might engage in masturbatory behavior whenever his anger or sexual feelings are aroused. In other words, it is the child's anxiety, combined with an avoidance of feeling (these youngsters rarely understand or know what they are feeling) that leads to regressive or any other defensive behavior.

In general, it is important to understand the psychological purpose of regression in order to learn what to do about it. If foster parents recognize that regression serves a purpose—namely, to reduce anxiety and control impulses—they are less likely to try to simply force the child to stop the regressive behavior. Nonetheless, they want to help the child discontinue inappropriate behavior, and much regressive behavior falls under this category. The important question for foster parents, therefore, is how to help a child reduce or extinguish the inappropriate, regressive behavior while helping him maintain his feelings of security and not overwhelming his fear. Essentially, there are two components to this process. First, and most important, the parents must begin to help the child recognize and understand his feelings and express them verbally. Verbal expression of feelings is more age appropriate and can help a child reduce anxiety and thereby reduce regressive behavior. Second, it is preferable not to focus on the regressive behavior itself but to look to the feelings that contribute to that behavior.

Let us explain these in more detail. For a youngster who shows many signs of fidgetiness and nervousness throughout the day and has numerous accidents wetting his pants, focusing on the wetting is not encouraged. Simply have the child change his clothes and clean himself up. Then focus on the nervousness and fidgetiness, and try to get the youngster to talk about his feelings. For example, the foster parents can say to the child something like, "You sure do seem nervous." At another time, especially when the foster parents observe the child in a situation in which someone else might feel angry, but the foster child is showing signs of nervousness, the parents might say something like, "Sometimes it makes you feel nervous when you don't express your anger," or, "It's okay to say why you are angry," or, "If I do something that makes you angry, I sure would like you to tell me about it." All these statements reflect the belief that it is okay to express anger and other feelings verbally and that talking about anger and feelings can reduce anxiety. By focusing on reducing the anxiety, parents will help the child reduce the unwanted behavior. Thus, the two key components of this approach are ignoring the regressive behavior itself and focusing on the feelings that contribute to the behavior.

Another component that helps some children is to help them understand that there is a reason for their regressive behavior. The foster parent should try and explain the connection between the inhibition of feelings and the regressive behavior. For example, at some point the foster parent could say to the child, "You know, sometimes I think that when you don't tell people how you feel, you're more likely to wet your pants," or, "Sometimes when you seem very nervous because you keep you feelings inside, you seem to be sucking your thumb more." By helping the child integrate feelings and behaviors in a cognitive way, parents can help him further reduce his regressive behavior. This is not automatic, and it will probably take some time, but many children benefit from understanding the relationship between their unwanted behaviors and their emotions. In many ways, such understanding can assist all children in reducing their use of unconscious behaviors to deal with their emotions. The foster child in particular, however, can gain tremendous reassurance and support from knowing that a loving adult understands the reasons why he does things that he may not want to continue doing.

Aggressiveness and Problems with Authority

Destructive behavior is often the most difficult behavior that foster parents must contend with. While many foster parents can tolerate expressions of anger and even occasional temper outbursts, it is extremely difficult for most to tolerate the destruction of their property or anything else. In this context, destructiveness is defined essentially as any act by which the child breaks or destroys property, as well as aggressive outbursts such as hitting, kicking, and fighting. It includes all expressions of anger in which an object or person takes the brunt of the anger. This does not include temper tantrums in which a child yells, screams, or whines, or other behavior that is not an action against some object or person. Such temper tantrums would be categorized as regressive behavior.

The main source of this destructiveness or aggressive behavior is poor impulse control. The child feels very angry and has major aggressive impulses but cannot control them behaviorally. Since anger is a common feeling associated with placement away from home, aggressive impulses are often overwhelming to the child. The child gets frustrated at some experience and acts destructively or aggressively toward some object with no control. Although this is a rather simplistic explanation for why foster children act in a destructive manner, the major components are nonetheless anger, frustration, and a lack of impulse control. Further discussion of such anger is beyond the scope of this book, but it is nonetheless important to look at how to deal with it.

Foster parents find it difficult to deal with aggressive and destructive behavior on the part of a foster child for several reasons. One reason is that their treatment of children in their care is bound by licensing regulations. Foster parents are prohibited to use even mild physical discipline by the licensing requirements of most states. No parent should physically abuse a child, and spanking for destructive or aggressive behavior is rarely the best response, but foster parents are often tempted to do so. But this common though somewhat inappropriate behavior is automatically excluded from the repertoire of disciplinary responses available to foster parents.

Another problem is that most people, as children, were probably spanked as a way of punishing destructive or aggressive behavior. Since people's actions as parents are largely influenced by the way they were treated by our own parents, foster parents might not know what to do when a particular form of punishment that they might choose is not available. Consequently, it is critical for foster parents to develop alternative disciplinary responses for a foster child who is aggressive and/or destructive.

According to psychological learning theory, it is easier to extinguish a behavior by ignoring it than by punishing it. This means that if parents want to decrease aggressive and/or destructive behavior, it is best for them to ignore it. This rationale was used in our discussion of regressive behaviors, but destructive and/or aggressive behavior is often very difficult to ignore.

Yet the very act of responding by disciplinary action actually positively reinforces the behavior. In other words, simply by responding to the aggressive and/or destructive behavior, parents are providing a reinforcement that will increase the likelihood that the child will continue this behavior. While this is somewhat complicated, it means that any disciplinary response could lead to an increase in destructive behavior rather than a decrease, which is what we want to see. In fact, one reason we do not want to use physical responses, such as spanking, is because the child is more likely to model the adult's behavior, and the spanking will reinforce further aggressiveness. Thus, there are both licensing and psychological reasons not to spank. Because parents do not want to reinforce aggressive or destructive behavior, they must find alternative ways to respond to a child's destructive and/or aggressive behavior.

We can find these alternatives in our discussion in Chapter 2 on rules and consistency. The child's aggressive or destructive behavior requires a response of some kind, so parents are likely to see—at least temporarily—some aggressiveness simply because of the fact that they are responding. But in choosing a response that consistently discourages destructiveness, provides an alternative, and states a fundamental belief that the child is allowed to feel angry, we can help shape a child's aggressive responses to more age-appropriate, less destructive, and less aggressive behavior. By helping the child learn to *stop and think* before she acts, parents can hopefully reduce her impulsive behavior, and by nurturing her right to feel angry about things and express her feelings, parents can train her to develop better ways of responding to all her feelings. The key components of this action are:

1. Stopping the child's destructiveness in a strong but benign way, as soon as possible
2. Providing a consistent message that the destructiveness is unacceptable but the feelings are acceptable
3. Providing an alternative behavior for the child that is acceptable

Let us examine these three components separately in more detail. The first component, stopping the behavior, is a critical step in helping to reduce impulsiveness. Remember, the child is impulsive and cannot stop the behavior himself. Lacking internal controls, he must rely on external controls to guarantee that the behavior will be stopped. This very important principle is helpful to remember, namely, the foster child does not necessarily want to act aggressively, but he lacks the internal control to prevent himself from acting aggressively and to behave in a socially more acceptable manner. He lacks the control because he has been abused or neglected, because he has watched others be violent and perhaps even be rewarded for this violence, or because of other psychological pathology. Since the child lacks this internal control, the foster parents provide control by physically restraining him whenever he begins to act in a destructive manner. The *consistent* application of physical restraint in response to a child's destructive behavior is *safe* (it does not include a negative physical response); it enhances a sense of *security* within the child; and it *stops the destructiveness* all at the same time. If applied on a consistent basis, it is benign toward the child and it is nurturing in the way it provides security. Since the child's destructive behavior is being controlled, he will actually be comforted by the physical restraint of the foster parent.

Restraint is accomplished in the following way. Imagine that you are a foster parent and are in a room with a seven-year-old foster child who is beginning to get very angry at you. In his anger, he comes to hit you. The most appropriate behavior for you at that moment is to take his hands and hold them so that he is unable to hit. By physically restraining him, you are providing him security, comfort, and a control of his impulses that he is unable to do himself. He is likely to argue that you are hurting him, scream at you, and otherwise make it seem as if you are committing the worst crime in the world. But at another level, he feels safer and more secure because his impulses are being externally controlled. It is important for you to restrain the child until he calms down sufficiently that he stops the aggressive behavior. Clearly, not every act of aggression requires restraint, but restraint is most useful in a situation in which it can help prevent destructive or aggressive action. Similarly, if a child goes to break something, attempt to restrain her before she does, if it is an item of value rather than simply a toy, which is less important. This restraint is not easy, and it requires a great deal of stamina and persistence to hang on while the child continues the destructive and aggressive efforts. Yet it is the most effective way to extinguish destructive behavior because it is immediate, and in most instances it will prevent the loss of control. In so doing, it helps the child to internalize the ability to control himself.

Restraint alone, however, is not sufficient to wholly extinguish such behavior. Other responses can lead to the reduction of aggressive and destructive behavior, such as telling the child that her behavior is unacceptable while reinforcing that her feelings are acceptable. This can be done essentially in two ways. While restraining the youngster, state consistently a message such as "When you are angry you cannot hit," or "Hitting is not allowed in this family." The second way is to impress on the child that she needs to *stop and think* before acting impulsively when she is angry. By saying something like, "When you are angry, stop and think. Hitting isn't acceptable, but telling me that you are angry is." Since many aggressive children have problems with impulse control, this is a very important message to clearly indicate to the child that she cannot act in a destructive or aggressive way. The application of physical restraint and the message to think before acting can help the child develop more self-control. Verbally stating the rule reinforces the inner development of self-control. Verbal skills utilize a higher level of psychological functioning than impulsive physical skills. By consistently modeling verbal skills in the presence of aggressive behavior and angry feelings, parents can help foster children learn to develop and use their own verbal skills rather than impulsively acting out.

This leads to the final step of the process. It is important to tell the child about alternative behaviors which are acceptable when the child is angry, both during but also after the aggressive behavior. While restraining the youngster, parents may say something such as, "Even though you are angry, you can't hit, but you can tell me how angry you feel," or, "When you feel this angry, you can tell me that you want to hit, but you can't hit."

Some people advocate telling a child that it is acceptable to hit an object, such as a pillow or punching bag. That behavior is in fact a better alternative to hitting a person or destroying something. If parents are trying to redirect a child's behavior from aggressive and destructive to verbal, telling the child he can hit a punching bag or a pillow is a good intermediate step along the way. After he begins to do this, parents can then encourage verbal skills. But a concern about this approach is that according to recent research, hitting objects does not sufficiently help a child improve his impulse control, and in its own way, it reinforces physical, destructive aggression.

This is where it is important to remember the goals of foster parenting. Foster parents are not just looking to help shape the behavior of a child who has a reasonable degree of impulse control. Rather, most foster children who act in a violent or destructive manner lack internal self-control. In other words, the important point is to do everything to help the child develop a greater degree of self-control. Hence, I do not recommend telling a child that it is acceptable to hit a punching bag or a pillow when angry. If a child who has been aggressive toward people begins to act aggressively toward acceptable objects, I would recommend that parents say something like, "I know that you're angry and I'm glad that you hit your pillow instead of me, even though you may have felt like hitting me. But I'd still prefer it if you could tell me that you're angry instead of hitting anything." Such a statement encourages the verbal expression of anger, which is the higher level of psychological functioning that parents are seeking.

It *is* recommended to tell a child that it is acceptable to hit a pillow or other such object when the child is one who essentially overinhibits most of her feelings and has no way of expressing her anger. Some children seem like time bombs waiting to explode. They are not yet in a position to be physically aggressive. By providing them with the security of striking a safe object, especially a punching bag, parents can help them reduce this overinhibition of feelings, and they can learn that there *are* acceptable ways of expressing angry feelings. In addition, since such children usually maintain their self-control, they can more easily be shaped to a more acceptable verbal expression of their feelings. Essentially, therefore, if a child has little or no inner self-control, parents should not encourage *any* physical expression of aggression but should help him develop as much inner self-control as possible. But for children who are overinhibited and need to be encouraged to relax their inhibitions somewhat, helping them to become *safely* physical in their expression of anger can be useful.

It is important to recognize that this process only works for children up to the age of ten or eleven. Certainly, by adolescence, it is very difficult for a foster parent to use physical restraint. The adolescent is more capable of hurting the foster parent than a younger child. Professionally, it is my opinion that overaggressive adolescents who lack sufficient internal self-control should be placed not in individual family foster homes but in group care settings. If an adolescent foster child does become physically aggressive, it may be necessary to call the police to provide the physical restraint. It is important to keep some distance from aggressive adolescents but to try to verbally reinforce the messages that destruction is unacceptable and that expressing feelings is acceptable, and that there are behaviors that are appropriate and acceptable when angry. If the adolescent is only rarely or minimally aggressive, he *can* be maintained in the family foster home. But if his aggressive actions become worse or if the foster parent cannot help him to develop some inner self-control, he needs to enter into a group care setting of some kind.

Many foster children have difficulty with authority figures of all kinds. This difficulty shows up in the foster home, at school, and in the community. In many ways, it is an extension of the child's anger and aggressiveness, but it also reflects her trouble in identifying with a healthy adult in early life. Typically, most children learn to respect adults and authority figures through the positive bonding that takes place within the family. By identifying with the parent, children take on traits of the parent and respect the adults who make them feel good. But because of the abuse and neglect that most foster children have felt, they have much less ability to respect or interest in respecting authority. It takes time for these children to develop the kind of respect that parents may want, but by taking the approach discussed here, parents may be able to get the child at least to respond to authority in a more positive way. As with lying and stealing, it is important to not take this personally but rather to help the child understand the reasons for this behavior while subtly encouraging more appropriate behavior toward authority figures.

Sibling Problems

Issues with foster siblings are not essentially different from issues with siblings in general. Children set up rivalries with one another when they feel less loved than a sibling, and they attribute the reason for this lack of love either to themselves or to a parent. But foster care can complicate the typical sibling rivalry for several reasons.

First, children who enter foster care already have a poor self-image and believe that the reason they have been treated poorly is because of a fault within themselves. When the foster child transfers this belief to the new situation, he sets up situations that he thinks show that he is being treated poorly in comparison with a sibling (meaning his own biological sibling, a foster sibling, or a biological child of the foster parent). He may set up conflicts with foster siblings in which he will always lose, or he may create lots of problems for this foster sibling for which he gets into trouble. He uses this to reinforce his belief that he is bad or that he is inadequate in comparison with others.

A second reason for complications is that the foster sibling is placed among siblings who are the biological children of the foster parent. This situation need not create difficulties, but it can when one of two things happens. Either the foster parents truly favor the biological child and treat her better than the foster child, or foster parents overcompensate for their partiality toward their biological child, reduce their favoritism toward her, and favor the foster child. In either case, affection, love, attention, and nurturance to the children involved are distributed unevenly. If the foster parents give more to their own child, the foster child resents it and may use this to justify his own belief that he is bad and doesn't deserve any more.

On the other hand, if the foster child is favored, the biological child will develop resentment and may attempt to get the foster child into trouble. In either case, one child or the other will feel that the uneven distribution of "love" is unfair and will develop feelings of resentment.

Finally, sibling problems are also complicated in foster care when two or more foster children from the same biological family come into a foster home. In this situation, it is quite common that the older child has a history of taking care of the younger child in their original family group. Many older siblings were in the role of primary caretaker due to a psychologically or physically absent parent. Once the siblings are placed in foster care, adults generally expect that children as children will look to the adults for love, nurturance, and rules. But in these circumstances, the younger child will look to her older biological sibling first. This can lead to conflicting messages from the differing authority figures, and it will be harder for the foster children to develop a natural bond with the foster parents. The older foster child, moreover, perceives himself in more of an adult role and finds it hard to accept the nurturance and love offered by the foster parents. He is so unused to nurturance and love that he cannot accept it in the foster home. This can lead to feelings of alienation in both the foster child and the foster parent, as well as associated feelings of resentment.

It is important for foster parents to recognize the possibility that such sibling difficulties will arise and act in ways that might reduce them. For example, if a foster child or a biological child feels some resentment due to uneven distribution of love, it is important for parents to recognize that the foster child is likely to attribute the unfairness to his own inadequacy. Thus, foster parents can make statements that reinforce feelings of adequacy within the child. Saying things such as, "I'm glad to have you in our family," or, "You really do that great," can counteract feelings of inadequacy. If two biologically related foster children enter the foster home together, it might be best for the foster parent to stay back a little bit at first and watch the evolution of the roles among the foster children. When the foster parents become aware of these roles, they can assert their own authority with the younger foster child, while trying to provide some nurturance and mild independence to the older child. It is critical for foster parents to be aware of the reasons foster children act as they do, so that they do not develop feelings of resentment or alienation toward the foster children.

The Passive-Aggressive Child

Another common problem among foster children is the passive-aggressive child. The passive-aggressive child is generally very quiet, passive, and indecisive, behavior that evokes an angry response from others. A foster parent will not feel angry most of the time toward a quiet, shy, but pleasant child. But if a foster parent who rarely feels angry toward children in general feels generally angry toward a passive child, the child maybe passive aggressive.

In many ways, passive aggressive children are much more difficult to deal with than actively aggressive ones. Parents know why they have the feelings they do toward actively aggressive children. They act aggressively toward the parents, they might break things or hit at the parents, and they actively elicit anger with their own anger. But it is normally difficult for foster parents to understand why they feel anger toward passive-aggressive children. The passive-aggressive child cannot express anger in any way except by passive, indecisive non-action but in general he is extremely angry. He overinhibits the anger because he fears expressing it and needs for others to get angry at him. Then, when others get angry at him, he is reinforced in the belief that he is bad.

In a typical encounter with a passive-aggressive child, the parent might ask, "Where do you want to go for dinner?" A mildly indecisive child might have a hard time deciding but will usually make a decision if given enough choices and is generally pleasant while exploring the choices. By contrast, a passive-aggressive child is likely to be negative toward every choice offered, offer no acceptable alternatives, and almost have a sneer on his face throughout the process. Essentially, she is eliciting anger from you with her own generalized angry style. For the most part, there is only one effective way for the foster parent to deal with her passive-aggressive behavior: that is to recognize the reasons for her anger and ignore her passive-aggressiveness. Make decisions for the child, take away her rights to assert herself or be active, and ignore the irrelevant behavior. In addition, parents can begin to allow the child to actively express some of her angry feelings in an appropriate manner, although many passive-aggressive children deny that they are angry. In fact, the only way for the foster parent to reveal the anger is to take away the passive-aggressive "defense" or to act in a reasonably aggressive, assertive way himself. Therapy for the child is another effective means of dealing with this behavior.

Truancy, School Phobia, and Learning Problems

Many foster children come into foster care with some type of learning and/or school problems. Many of these kids have received little or no encouragement in their school activities. Many have specific learning problems due to environmental, emotional, and/ or physiological factors. Younger children may be afraid of school, afraid of separation, and afraid of strangers. Older children may skip school, run away, or feel hopeless at school. These and other problems are common for children in foster care. If a child comes into foster care and little information about his schooling is available, it is important for the foster parents to talk with school officials about the expected needs of the child. For the first few weeks, when the foster parents, teacher(s), and other school officials are beginning to gain an understanding of the child and his academic needs, the most important thing is to observe the child in school and try to understand as much as possible about her learning style, fears, and behaviors in school with teachers and peers. This information will be the foundation for understanding later, if things begin to change.

When school problems first arise, it is important to try to determine the source of the problem. Various behaviors can result from emotional factors, but at school there are other possible causes as well. Some children's learning disabilities are due to emotional and/or physical factors that may impair their ability to learn in a regular classroom setting. If such a disability exists, the children may be aggressive, afraid, unresponsive, bored, truant, or depressed. Thus, adults cannot tell from one symptom alone what the nature of the school problem is. Instead, they need a thorough psychological and academic evaluation of the child to help determine the nature and degree of a possible learning disability. Such an evaluation can usually help the foster parents distinguish between the physical and emotional causes of such disabilities, and they can use that information to help develop a remedial plan for the child. When the evaluation process is complete, the foster parents, social workers, and school personnel can meet together to determine the appropriate planning for the child. Some children will need special tutoring; others will need therapy; many will need special education classes and/or medication to help. A smaller percentage of children may need assistance in several of these areas. The key point is that the evaluation is necessary to understand the source of the school problems, and it is used to provide direction for solving the problems.

I'd like to offer a few words about school phobia, truancy, and/or school refusal in young children. Psychological research suggests that the cause of these problems is often fear of separation and emotional difficulties related to anger and poor relationships with parents. Foster children commonly show symptoms of school phobia, school refusal, or truancy for these same reasons. They are angry at their parents, they have been hurt, they feel aggressive inside, and they are afraid that new authority figures may hurt them. When children don't understand these feelings, they are confused and may develop the symptoms. A combination of nurturance in the foster home, firmness that the child *must* attend school, and therapy is usually necessary to solve this type of school problem. Typically, school phobia will settle down rather quickly with this approach, but therapy will be necessary for quite a while to help the child with the emotions that underlay these problems.

Drug-dependent Children

A growing problem in the past few years has been drug-dependent children, most of whom come into foster care as infants. Usually, the drug usage of the pregnant mother causes the infant to be removed from the mother at birth by protective services and the hospital. Drug-dependent infants require a great deal of patience, medical support, and care in the first few months of their life to help them overcome the effects of drug dependence. Most of these babies are given to specialists in such foster care, and the foster parents work closely with medical personnel to develop special routines that help the child regain a normal course of development. Many of these babies are born premature and stay in the hospital for several weeks while undoing the immediate effects of the drug dependency.

After leaving the hospital, many of these infants require special feeding techniques, sleep routines, and ongoing medical care that require nearly twenty-four-hour-per-day assistance. The temperaments of drug-dependent babies are often very difficult. Many of them cry a great deal, no matter what the parents do to meet their physical and other needs. Caring for them is very demanding and requires a special commitment. Parents who take such foster children should not feel burdened already, as this could make it difficult for them to provide the necessary care to the child. It is critically important that the foster parents of these children know their own limitations and not allow an overburdened system to overburden them. Once someone accepts such a foster child, they are easily perceived as someone who can handle and deal with the needs and demands of difficult children, and the tendency on the part of the system is to place another such child in that home due to the previous "success". A foster parent who is prepared to handle the challenge and commitment again may do it, but if not, he or she should not hesitate to assert their own needs for time away from such demands. No child is easy to raise, but these drug-dependent, often difficult babies frequently cause burnout in an already overburdened population of foster parents.

Drug and Alcohol Abuse

Many children come into foster care as the direct or indirect result of drug or alcohol abuse by their parents. Children who have lived in homes of drug-using parents, are at a higher risk themselves for use and/or abuse of drugs when they grow up. There are three major reasons for this.

First, such children may feel that drug use is acceptable because they have lived with it for so long. Even if they recognize that they were removed from home due to the drug abuse of their parent(s), they may not fully understand that there is any significant problem with the use of drugs, and they may see it as perfectly acceptable behavior. Obviously, these children require a great deal of education on the dangers of drug and alcohol abuse so as to minimize their risk for future use.

The second reason is the fact that many foster children have a poor self-image, do poorly in school, and see themselves as failures in life. Since they are depressed and may have no hope for the future, they are more susceptible to pressure from peers who are "into" drugs and alcohol. Drugs and alcohol provide a way to numb one's painful feelings, and the sense of pleasure and relief of pain they provide feel good for a little while. Like everyone who gets "hooked" on drugs or alcohol, they become emotionally and/or physically dependent on the substance.

In addition, there is evidence that many foster children of drug-abusing parents may turn to drugs themselves as a form of identification with the missing parent. Drug use may allow the child to unconsciously feel closer to the parent, and it may reinforce his guilt feelings and feelings of how "bad" he thinks he is. The child does not understand such usage of drugs and/or alcohol, or that it is unconsciously related to other emotional symptoms.

For all children and especially foster children who have grown up in drug-abusing families, education and emotional well-being are the key factors in whether they are likely to abuse drugs. It is

important for foster parents to try to provide special drug education, if it is available in their community, such as through the
schools and/or police agencies. In many communities in the country, the program called DARE (drug abuse resistance education)
provides an excellent understanding of the problems of drugs and
education about ways to resist the use of drugs. Research suggests
that that program is most effective when taught by police agencies
and that it may be the most effective program in the country in
helping children who are at risk learn to resist the use of drugs
when they get older.

For children who show an unconscious emotional draw to
drugs, outpatient therapy may also be indicated. While there is
less evidence that therapy reduces the risk of drug use, it may
reduce depression and improve self-image so that drugs are less
appealing. In addition, for children who unconsciously take drugs
to deal with conflicts in their relationships with their birth parents,
therapy can help them draw the connection to this behavior and
find other means of resolving their feelings about their parents and
their drug abuse. Finally, it is critical for those who are already
abusing substances to get help immediately from a well-staffed
and well-trained drug treatment program that can address and
deal with the physical, emotional, and educational issues related
to drug and alcohol abuse.

Sexually Abused/Abusive Children

The sexual behavior of foster children is increasingly a problem in
foster homes. Many foster children are sexually abused before
coming into foster care and, it is reported, by other foster children
while in care as well. This is especially true of children who have
been in residential treatment programs for some time. Much of the
increasing sexual acting out of young children is the direct and
indirect result of the sexual abuse and/or sexualized experiences
that the children experienced before coming into foster care.

Sexual play between children is generally considered "normal"
when the two children are of similar age and it is limited to behaviors that are seen as "age appropriate." Looking at or touching
body parts is considered typical for three- to seven-year-old chil-

dren when done in private, with consent, and between children of the same age, regardless of whether they are of the same or different sex. Similarly, masturbation and bathroom or sexual humor are considered age appropriate if not overdone.

But foster parents grow concerned when sexual play appears to mimic adult sexual behavior or becomes excessive or forced, or if it involves children of significantly different ages. It may initially take the simple form of one child climbing into another child's bed, but the evidence is that all too frequently, young children are engaging in confusing and sexually inappropriate behavior. This behavior can include, but is not limited to, a child touching another child's private parts, exposing himself to others, being sexually provocative toward peers and/or adults, and exhibiting much sexual talk and/or play (such as mimicking sexual behavior with a doll or stuffed animal). A common form of inappropriate sexualized play is for one child to attempt or request oral sex with another child, even if the children are the same age. Whenever the sexual play is "uncommon"—that is, is likely the result of the child witnessing or experiencing adult sexual behavior—it is probably the result of sexual abuse that has been suffered by the child or of much overt sexual overstimulation in the biological home. Foster parents have a very difficult time knowing how to deal with such behavior, and it is a common reason that they ask that a child be placed into another home.

Rather than ask that the child be moved, however, it might be useful for foster parents to try to set limits and rules regarding sexualized behavior. Telling the child that he cannot expose himself or engage in such sexualized play and then monitoring his behavior can be quite useful. Teaching children that such behavior is "inappropriate" in the family, while teaching about sex in general, can also help. Providing a structure that allows the foster parents to better monitor a child's behavior and that rewards the child for nonsexual behavior can also help reduce these symptoms. Finally, therapy can help these children work out difficulties in their feelings about the way they were treated sexually and can be the most effective way to reduce these behaviors. As long as foster parents set limits and do not overreact to the sexually acting out child, things should settle down after a period of time. But it is important for foster parents to recognize that some sexual acting out, like some aggressive acting out, can be controlled only in group care or in residential treatment settings. In these cases it is important to try and work out the difficulties first and resort to a different placement only after monitoring and structuring efforts have failed.

Foster Children Having Babies

A final problem whose incidence is on the rise in foster care is the pregnancy of foster teenagers. Teenage pregnancy is on the rise in all segments of the population, but it is of special difficulty for the foster care population. The biggest questions are whether the pregnant teen can remain in the foster home and whether the foster parents wish to care for the baby after the pregnancy.

When a teenage ward of the court gives birth to a baby, the baby is automatically a ward of the court in most states and is therefore subject to the possibility of foster care placement. Sometimes mother and baby are placed together, and sometimes they are split apart. This largely depends on the foster parents' willingness to care for the baby or to monitor the care that the baby receives from the mother.

As one can imagine, making the decisions about all of this is quite tricky. For the most part, it is best if the teenage mother and her baby can be placed together in a nurturing setting, where she can learn how to care for her baby under the teaching and direction of the foster mother. This is best not only because it helps the new mother learn to be a "good enough" mother, but also because taking the new baby away from the mother reinforces her belief that she is "bad" and assumes that mothers cannot learn to be responsible and care for their babies. All too often, teenage foster girls get pregnant to reenact their own failed relationships with their mothers and to make it right this time. By arranging a placement in which the new mother can be with and care for her child and learn to do it right, the foster care system can help the foster child have a necessary corrective experience. Only when the new mother is quite irresponsible and immature might it be wise to place the baby in a separate foster home where it will have an opportunity for attachment and bonding on its own.

This chapter has outlined a number of the typical and more significant problems in foster parenting. They include, but are not limited to: lying, stealing, regressive behaviors, destructive and aggressive behaviors, sibling difficulties, passive aggressiveness, school problems, drug and alcohol problems, sexual abuse and sexual acting out, and foster children having babies. This chapter has tried to explain the sources of these problems and has also provided ways to deal with them. Most important, foster parents need to recognize that most of the inappropriate behavior is the result of the foster child's earlier experiences of abuse and neglect. If they can remember that simple fact, they will find it easier to approach the child's behavior with specific techniques rather than with feelings of inadequacy or anger. By separating out the foster parent's feelings from the behavioral techniques, they can do a better job of responding to the foster child's behavior.

6

Working with Systems

IN addition to dealing with the day-to-day behavior of the foster child, meeting all his needs, and helping him with his problems, foster parents have another major task as well. This task is less talked about but is equally important for the welfare of the child. Again, understanding the task can make it much easier. This task consists of working with the variety of systems outside the foster home that are critical to the foster child's life. These systems essentially include the foster care agencies (and/or child protective service agencies), the schools, medical and psychological consultants, the courts, and the biological parents. Although there is mild overlap between these systems, this chapter examines each one individually.

Foster Care Agencies

Probably the most important system that foster parents need to work with is the foster care agency, and possibly the child protective service agency. What we discuss in relation to the foster care agency is equally applicable to the child protective service agency. The work that a foster parent must do in relation to the foster agency varies from state to state and agency to agency, but essentially, certain tasks are expected of foster parents. The primary job of the foster parents in relation to the agency is to work with the agency for the welfare of the child. This means many things. First, the foster parents need to heed the suggestions that the social workers make regarding discipline and scheduling. The agency staff is aware of the overall needs and plans for the child, but foster parents are not always aware of the complete plan. It is essential that the work of the foster parents be integrated with the rest of the child's foster care plan, and this requires complete communication between the foster parents and the social workers to guarantee that everyone is doing a good job of meeting all the child's needs.

In addition to listening to the agency staff and taking suggestions from them, it is critical that foster parents keep a dialogue going with agency staff about the child and her progress in the foster home. Typically, foster parents meet with a social worker on a regularly scheduled basis to discuss the child's progress. At those meetings, it is important to talk about both the strengths of and the problems in the foster home. Foster parents and social workers tend to avoid discussing minor problems, believing they are unimportant. But they are often the first signs of potential major problems, and discussing and understanding them early can help keep them from evolving into bigger problems. Just as important to discuss, however, are the mild strengths of the child that the foster parents notice. All too often, only the foster child's problems are discussed, which lowers everyone's confidence and reduces confidence in the foster care plan. By looking at the child's strengths and weaknesses, everyone can better understand the complete child and her overall progress and adjustment. Then foster parents can feel better about their work and get a more accurate picture of the child's overall functioning. As such, it is important to view the foster parent–foster agency relationship as a co-working relationship, in which each part of the team has a different job. Even though the jobs are different, there is still one primary goal toward which both are working; namely, helping the welfare of the child. Foster parents and agency staff working together can best help the interests of the child and seek to reach the goals which have been developed.

Several problems occasionally develop in the foster parent–agency relationship. One is that the agency staff does not always adequately communicate the goals to the foster parent. If the social worker does not inform the foster parents of the goals of foster care, it is difficult for the foster parents to do a thorough job. The best thing for foster parents to do is to ask the social worker about the goals and how they can help implement the goals. They should also try to get as detailed a description of the child's background as possible. Foster parents don't need to know everything about the child's background, but they need to know enough to help them understand problems that may develop. They need to actively participate in understanding the child and her needs while in foster care.

Schools

It is also important for the foster parents to recognize their relationship with the school. Although the foster care agency may work closely with the school, the foster parents are essentially the first-line communicators of the academic strengths and problems of the child. Foster parents reinforce schoolwork and help the child learn good study habits; schools and foster parents must work together to set up plans to help the child do well in school. Many foster children have never attended school regularly, and they were never encouraged to do schoolwork. Foster care is the first opportunity for these children to learn appropriate school behaviors and study habits. Foster parents should maintain a dialogue with the school to find out if the child has homework and to learn more about the school's expectations; in turn, they can help the school know more about the child's work habits.

Many foster children do not do homework assignment. Foster parents can work with the school and the child to structure the child's homework time. A typical plan could be as follows. The foster parent should first determine the amount of homework the child is doing and the number of assignments he is turning in, if any. If he is doing none, the parent and the teacher talk and together realize that the child is saying there is no homework even though the teacher is assigning homework. A child who has been doing no homework and turning in no assignments should be told that from now on he should take papers home and have the parents initial them. This shows the teacher that the parent has received the paper and knows that there was an assignment. When there is no homework assignment, the teacher will also send a note home.

Thus, the parent can expect to get a note every day from the teacher. This eliminates the opportunity for the child to continue saying that there is no homework.

Next, the parent and child work together to develop a schedule that will reward the child in some way for doing homework. The best possible rewards are activities in which the child likes to participate, such as watching TV. For example, after a one half-hour period of doing homework, the child can watch one half-hour of TV. The key to using rewards is that they are applied every time the child engages in the activity. This is the best way for the child to learn a preferred new behavior.

The next step in the process is that when the child completes an assignment, the parent initials it before the child takes it to the teacher. The teacher, too, should receive something every day from the parent—either a statement that the assignment is not complete or the assignment itself. Under this arrangement, parent and teacher both continuously know what is being accomplished. Finally, after the new behavior is well established, the parent can change the reward to something that the child values even more and then periodically reward the child with this. A trip to the ice cream store, a new toy, or a similar activity or treat can be the new reward, to be applied on a periodic basis. By setting up a schedule that rewards the child periodically, parents can help to maintain the valued behavior that has already been learned.

Essentially, the principles of behavioral psychology explain how people learn new tasks. Any process that gets the parent and teacher to work together so that rewards positively valued by the child can be applied consistently will assist in the learning. An initial schedule in which the reward is regular and frequent, followed by a schedule that is more variable, seems to work best. Finally, the child should be aware of and a part of this process, because motivation appears to contribute to the process, as well.

Courts

Foster parents are generally insulated from the court process. Protective services, social service agencies, social workers, and biological parents are all involved with the courts, but it is fairly rare for the foster parents to get involved. On occasion, however, foster parents are asked to participate as witnesses of the child and his relationship with the biological parents. Parents become involved if the court is considering terminating parental rights, and the foster parents can be witnesses to specific behaviors that they observed between the biological parents and the child. They may be called to describe phone calls they have seen, threats they have heard, or instances where parents have tried to physically abuse the child while in the foster parents' care. In addition, foster parents might see serious problems in the foster child after visits with the biological parents, and this may need to be communicated to the court. While all of this is rare, mostly because foster parents are usually insulated from the more chaotic biological parents, the courts are increasingly seeing foster parents as having expertise in understanding the foster child and her needs.

While foster parents' impact may be quite direct, when they are called as witnesses, foster parents typically have a more indirect impact upon the court system, when foster parents tell social workers about the interactions between the child and the biological parents. For example, if the foster parents note that after visits the foster child is doing better, talks positively about how the weekend went, and is generally improving relationship skills, they should communicate this because it may reflect improvement in the biological parents' functioning. But if the foster child comes back from weekends with signs of increased anxiety, increased sleep disturbances or bedwetting, or more aggressive behavior, this might reflect disturbances during the weekend and should also be noted by the foster parents. It is important for the foster parents to describe the behaviors to the social workers and work with them to determine the possible meaning of the changed behavior.

Any behavior change could reflect two opposite syndromes in foster care and thus requires close understanding. For example, if foster children come back from a weekend visit with increased anxiety, increased sleep disturbances, and increased aggression, it is common to assume that they have had difficulty due to birth parent dysfunction. But other foster children enjoy their weekend visits and may have had no problems; they may show such symptoms because of their anger at having to return to foster care. Increased anger, especially in a child who has not yet learned to tolerate this anger, can produce these same symptoms. Thus, foster parents need to describe the symptoms to the social workers and together, possibly with the help of therapists, understand their significance.

Biological Family

Another major system with which the foster parents must interact is the biological family. This interaction can occur on several levels. In the primary level, the foster child is in the middle. The foster child has attachments to both the foster parents and biological parents and as a result continually compares the foster parents and the biological parents with one another. Thus, while the foster parents do not interact directly with the biological parents, they have nonetheless an indirect interaction based upon the child's perceptions and feelings. This is especially true of foster children who feel ambivalent toward both their biological and their foster parents.

Other foster parents have limited telephone contact with biological parents. Biological parents are permitted to telephone the foster home on a timed, regular basis, and the foster parents engage in conversation with the biological parents during these calls. In general, it is usually best for foster parents to be polite, look for positive and negative cues in relation to the child, and stay out of controversy. These phone calls are meant to be between the biological parents and the child, and the best thing is for the foster parents to stay out of the middle as much as possible. If the foster parents see evidence that the child is getting upset during the phone call, they should not interrupt the phone call but should help the child with her anxieties and other feelings after the call is over. Giving cues to help the child end the call if she wants to can be potentially useful, such as reminding her that she has homework to do or something like that. It is important to communicate the anxiety that the child felt about the phone call to the social worker.

Many times, foster parents are asked to help other biological relatives visit the foster children, and this takes a lot of time. Aunts, uncles, and grandparents all want time with the child, and each of them may provide both a help and some problems. The task of the foster parents is to communicate to the social worker the needs and activities of the foster child and how these are affected by all the visits. Sometimes such visits occur almost every weekend, which may interfere with the child's adjustment to the community, to friends, and to new activities. The foster parents and the social worker should coordinate all these activities so that the child can make a good adjustment, feel a part of his community and his biological family, and not be overloaded. This is sometimes difficult, but it is a necessary task in helping the child adjust to the foster home.

Finally, foster parents and biological parents interact a great deal in many instances, especially when the foster child is beginning the process of returning home. Foster parents might drop the child off at the agency or at the biological parents' home, and the biological parents may pick the child up at the foster home. Especially in those instances when there is a degree of pleasantness between the foster parents and the biological parents, it is perfectly all right to engage in more conversation, but it is best to keep conversation limited around the child. Sometimes the biological parents try to use the foster parents to talk about a lot of different things, such as their life and their problems. This is very hard on the foster parents. Foster parents should gently, politely, but firmly refuse to engage in such supportive conversations with the biological parents unless the problems are very few and mostly centered on the child.

Finally, after a child returns to her biological home, the foster parents sometimes continue to be a resource and support to both the biological parents and to the foster child. In those instances, visits can be ongoing throughout the year. It can be very beneficial for the child adjusting to the return home to know that he need have no concern about having to give up his attachment to the foster parents. The continuing attachment is like that with an aunt or uncle, in which there are periodic visits and a lot of love and warmth, but no parental ties. In fact, this is the best way to help the child adjust to the return home, as it continues the stability of the relationship with the foster parents, who have been very important to the child's life.

Physicians, Dentists, and Psychologists

Another group of professionals in the community with whom the foster parents must also get to know and work with are the medical, dental, and therapeutic professionals. All foster children require medical and dental checkups and regular care, and many need some type of psychological evaluation or therapy. Foster parents are expected to take foster children to appointments whenever they are set by the foster care agency. These appointments can be at a variety of locations in the general vicinity of the foster home. Most often, the social workers set up the appointments based on the schedule of the professionals. Thus, foster parents who have special needs regarding scheduling should talk with the professionals and set these appointments accordingly.

In addition, foster parents may get a great deal of assistance by working with a local psychologist who understands the needs of emotionally deprived or damaged children. Thus, despite the work involved in transporting children to appointments and following through on medical, psychological, and dental treatments, these professionals can assist foster parents in better understanding their particular foster child and her needs. A local mental health professional can often be a valuable resource for working out specific problems before they get out of hand. Therapy is often an essential part of the foster care plan, and if more foster parents could use each other and their social workers to learn about therapists who understand the needs of foster children, more of these children might get the therapeutic help they frequently need.

This chapter has focused on the many professionals and systems in the community with which foster parents are often asked to interact. While not all foster parents will have significant contact with all of them, an understanding of the possible interactions and of the basic expectations can be quite helpful. In fact, it is most helpful for everyone to understand the expectations that others have of them, and that they have of ourselves and of others. The next chapter focuses on the expectations of foster parents and the relationship between these expectations and the overall foster care process.

7

Foster Parents' Expectations

FOSTER parents have various expectations of the way their foster children will relate to them and act in their home. These expectations arise from previous experiences with children, from foster parent training, and from awareness of the child's problems and behavior in previous foster homes. Foster parents have expectations about how their foster children will attach and form relationships, and about the length of time a child will remain in foster care. Each of these expectations plays a role in how foster parents relate to foster children, especially if problems develop that were not part of the expectations. If the experience of the placement differs markedly from the expectations the parents held before the child entered their care, the need may arise to move the child to a different placement. Typically, foster parents talk with their social workers to get help in understanding the problems that exist, but the parents often lack a framework in which to understand how their expectations can go awry and what to do about it. In this chapter, we will look closely at the original expectations in order to provide a framework to understand how foster parents can deal effectively with situations that differ from their original expectations.

Initial Expectations

One of the most common complaints foster parents make is that a child's behavior is unlike anything they have ever encountered in children they have previously raised. While this complaint is most commonly voiced by new foster parents, it is also heard from those who find that a particular foster child's behavior is more difficult than that of foster children previously encountered. It may present a great deal of difficulty when foster parents who were willing to take a child based on their expectation of how children act find that a child is acting in a way that is markedly different from those expectations. These foster parents might not really understand why a youngster is having some of the problems he is having, nor how to deal with the fears, vulnerabilities, or emotional stresses inherent in foster care. Foster care does work best in temporary circumstances, and it is often very difficult for children to come into a new home and act like other children their age. If the primary experience of the foster parents has been with biological children, they should begin to recognize how foster children act differently, at least early on. Understanding the typical process of a youngster's entry into foster care is helpful in resolving some of the difficulties around such expectations.

When a youngster first comes into foster care, there is typically a "honeymoon" in which everyone tries to get along. The foster child is somewhat frightened and, in feeling vulnerable, tries to please the foster parents all the time. This sets up a false expectation about how the foster care process will go thereafter. During the first few weeks or months, usually spent in this honeymoon atmosphere, the foster parents are quite happy with the initial transition, and the child develops an expectation that things will continue this way. The foster child and the foster parents generally get along quite well at this time.

Once the child settles in, however, and begins to trust his foster parents, problems often develop in his behavior or in other, more subtle ways. Foster parents need to take into account that in a child's typical transition into foster care, the child needs to test the new relationship. Foster parents need to provide some of the behavioral management techniques noted in Chapter 2.

Foster parents who recognize that new children will have some difficulty after the honeymoon is over find it easier to apply the behavioral management techniques. Foster parents with unrealistic expectations that the honeymoon will continue or that the child will simply begin to act like "normal" children at a certain age or in certain circumstances will create a great deal of tension for foster child and foster parent alike. Foster parents can refer back to the possible problems noted in Chapters 4 and 5 and recognize how foster children's emotions routinely affect some of their behaviors. In this way, they can begin to develop more realistic expectations that match the foster child's behavior.

Foster Parent Training

The training that foster parents receive will also affect their expectations of children in foster care. Some foster programs provide several weeks of training before foster parents get any foster children. Others provide only a limited amount of such training and very little information about what to expect. Training usually lasts several hours and covers the basics about child development, the foster care system, and what to expect from foster children. Foster parent training is sometimes part of the process by which social service agencies determine which parents are suitable for foster parenting. No matter what kind of training is offered, however, most foster parents feel that it is insufficient. Nonetheless, it usually leaves foster parents with a basic idea of what to expect and plays a significant role in foster parent expectations. To guarantee a better understanding and expectations of foster care, most foster parents are looking to professionalize foster parenting, and they encourage agencies to provide ongoing education and assistance in caring for and raising the more difficult foster children.

The Foster Child's Previous Behavior

Foster parents are often given some advance description of the children and their problems, but sometimes foster parents have receive no advance information about their prospective foster child except possibly the age and the sex of the child. Foster parents who are told nothing about the child develop no expectations until they get to know the child at least a little bit. They develop an understanding of the child through their own relationship and then develop expectations of the relationship and how to deal with the child.

But foster parents who have been told a lot about previous placements often have an automatic expectation as to how to deal with the child and how the child will act. Foster parents who have been told about previous problems of the child often expect that the child will have the same problems in their own home. There are clear and distinct advantages and disadvantages to discussing with the parents the child's behavior in previous foster homes or in his biological home.

The basic advantage of providing such information is that the foster parents know what to expect. If a foster child is a bedwetter or has destructive or behavioral problems, the foster parent will understand the problems and try to deal effectively with them. Foster parents who know of the typical day-to-day behavior of the child can be prepared with various parenting skills and techniques useful in helping the child with behavioral problems.

For example, if foster parents know that the child is likely to be aggressive, they can refer back to the chapter on destructive and aggressive behavior for a variety of parenting techniques that will hopefully reduce the aggressive and destructive behavior. Similarly, if the child engages in regressive behavior, foster parents who know this in advance will have a better understanding of why it arises and how to ignore some of the irrelevant behaviors. Providing the foster parents with some description of basic day-to-day behavior thus gives them an opportunity to be prepared for taking care of the child.

Another potential advantage of advance information is that foster parents will not feel as overwhelmed as they might otherwise. During the honeymoon period, children may act fairly reasonably, but if foster parents know of a history of problems, they can be on the lookout for them and not be shocked or overwhelmed when they occur after the honeymoon stage. By being prepared, the foster parents will be better able to deal with difficulties that may occur.

In order to fully take advantage of this, foster parents should be told not only of the worst possible behaviors but of the day-to-day functioning of the child. Foster parents need to know how clingy the child is, how demanding the child is, in what circumstances the child plays with peers, the child's functioning in school, the eating and sleeping habits of the child, the activity level of the child, and the mood of the child. In other words, the highlights alone are not sufficient for the foster parent to deal with the day-to-day behavior of the child. As much information as is available should be shared with prospective foster parents to give them a realistic expectation of how the child is likely to act and to enable them to be prepared for problems that could occur.

But it is important to bear in mind that there can also be disadvantages in providing this kind of information. First, no one can ever be sure how a child will function in a new environment based on previous functioning. For example, if a child was aggressive and destructive in a previous foster home, it could be related to the inadequate skills of the foster parents there. Similarly, if regressive behaviors occurred at home, they might disappear in the more stable environment of foster care. Behaviors and functions that are more transient and related to the environment may not be exhibited in a more stable, secure foster home.

Second, foster parents who have advance information about problems might be less likely to allow the relationship to unfold naturally because they have been forewarned. They may even inadvertently set up or encourage inappropriate behavior out of a fear or belief that it is ready to occur. Studies have shown that parents or teachers who expect misbehavior often subtly encourage misbehavior. Parents who expect foster children to act in a negative way may inadvertently cause this behavior to occur. A final disadvantage is that foster parents may unwittingly utilize parenting techniques that cause a foster child to continue his inappropriate behavior and thus reinforce the child's belief that he is bad.

The question becomes, therefore, how much information foster parents should have before a foster child comes into their care. Based on my own experience with a variety of foster families and foster children, my opinion is that there is no set guideline that will work in every case. Instead, it is important that the foster parents know themselves well enough to monitor their own needs and act in response to them. It is probably best for foster parents to be given a vague idea of the child's daily functioning without horror stories of what may happen. The foster parent needs to know if a child has exhibited serious difficulty in other foster homes to make an accurate decision as to whether the child would function in their home. This information need not alarm foster parents or worry them, but it will give them a sense of the actual impact the child will have. Parents who know themselves and are honest with themselves can best decide if they are truly prepared to work with a child who has the problems being presented to them.

On the other hand, it is also helpful to let the relationship unfold. Advance information, while important, must be tempered because of the need to let the parents and child get to know each other without the interference of knowledge and information from the past. The overall guidelines that I would recommend are that serious behavior problems should be forewarned, some basic awareness of daily functioning should be given, and the rest of the relationship needs to unfold between parents and child together. With this philosophy, it is extremely important that foster parents have available outside resources—agency personnel and ongoing foster parent training—that will enable them to deal with behaviors and problems that might arise. In addition, an open dialogue between foster parents and social service agency personnel can allow them to discuss problems and become more comfortable with the necessary parenting skills and techniques. Thus, it appears that providing a medium amount of information, combined with maintaining an ongoing and open dialogue about the child and her functioning, is the optimum solution in most cases.

Attachment and the Development of a Relationship

One of foster parents' most common complaints is that the child is unable to form a relationship with them. Many foster parents are under the illusion that the child will come to their home and immediately begin to form a "normal" parent/child–like relationship. They rarely expect that the foster child will call them "Mom" or "Dad," but foster parents often expect children to be somewhat affectionate, listen to the rules, and be a part of the family. They recognize that new foster children require some time to develop a relationship, but they often expect that a fairly substantial relationship will develop within a month or two after the child comes into foster care. They usually believe that this relationship will be similar to the relationship they have with their own children, though possibly not as intense. Thus, it is a rude awakening for them to discover that the foster child remains somewhat aloof and uninvolved in family activities and continues to act more like a boarder than a child within a family. Even when foster parents do everything they can to nurture a warm, parent/child relationship, foster children may remain relatively isolated from the family.

To help explain this, it is important to focus a bit on the development of the "normal" parent/child attachment. While there is some evidence that a physiological attachment begins during pregnancy and at delivery, there is no doubt that the process of psychological attachment begins at birth. This early process of attachment is commonly referred to as "bonding," and it reflects the psychological, symbiotic relationship that develops between the infant and its mother. The first three years of life see a strong development of the attachment, and a bond is formed between the infant or toddler and its parents that becomes the foundation for relationships in later life. Any significant impairment in this attachment process often makes it difficult for a child to form new relationships, which may hinder a child's ability to relate significantly to others later in life. This extremely close relationship is special to the child and her parents, and all future relationships depend upon the development of a close, bonding attachment between the child and her parents.

But it is hard for a foster child to develop a new relationship with his foster parents. Most often, there has been a significant breakdown in his attachment with his biological parents. There has usually been extreme chaos and disturbance in the first three years of his life, which can lead to impairment in his ability to form relationships. If a strong parent-child attachment has developed, the child feels a significant loss when he goes into foster care, a loss that often results in depression. This depression interferes with the formation of new relationships. Since a close attachment of child and parent requires a lengthy history and maturation, beginning at birth, it is unrealistic to expect a foster child to come into a new family and begin relating within that family as if that history existed.

What, then, can foster parents expect of their relationships with their foster children? First, foster parents can expect the development of a warm adult-child relationship. Children form relationships with teachers, aunts, uncles, and other significant adults in their lives every day, and so they can, too, with the foster parents. If foster parents do not push too hard, the foster child's aloofness will often dissipate over time, though the child may remain somewhat distant in comparison with biological children. If there is a defect in the child's relationship capacity, foster parents can expect one of two things. Either the foster child will remain extremely distant and fight all efforts on the part of the foster parents to relate, or the foster child will become extremely clingy and try to use the foster parents as surrogates in the attachment process. Many children alternate between these two behaviors, which is extremely disconcerting and frustrating for foster parents who do not understand this process. Over time, foster children often begin to develop a more affectionate relationship, especially if they are younger, when they become willing to accept the nurturance of foster parents.

For a child who has had a substantial relationship with biological parents and expects to return home, her primary psychological attachment will remain with her biological parents. If the foster parents are adaptable, it will be easier for them to let the child's behavior guide them in the degree to which the child will form a significant relationship with them.

Length of Time in Foster Care

Another major issue affecting the child's functioning in foster care is the length of time the child has been in foster care. Studies have shown that a child's average stay in "temporary" foster care is often as long as three to five years. Other studies have shown that children move an average of five times and sometimes as many as ten or twelve times before some permanence is established. All this takes a heavy toll on children and makes the job of foster parenting that much more difficult. In general, the longer a child has been in foster care and the more moves have taken place, the greater difficulty the child will have while in care.

One thing foster parents can do to help a child who has been in care for a long time is to initially be a bit detached and provide

cture rather than attempt to develop an attach-
ng attachments gets more difficult every time a
a new foster home, and it is much harder for parents
nable attachment with a foster child who has moved
. two years than with one who is first coming into
is difficult to generalize on this subject because some
ain in foster care for a long period of time for a variety
reasons. But it is my experience that it is harder for
form relationships with adults and peers when they
. in foster care and have moved a lot for more than two or
ars. These children may form superficial relationships, but
n very difficult for them to get very close to anyone for fear
of being hurt or rejected when they move again.

Ultimately, a very young child who has not yet formed a
significant attachment to his biological parents and who is placed
in foster care and then moved several times in several years will
likely end up with a markedly impaired ability to relate, irrespec-
tive of the work of foster parents. To offset this, the main thing that
foster parents can do is to remain foster parents to a particular
child for the entire time that the child is in foster care. The key to
this is *commitment*. By taking a foster child, foster parents are making a commitment to help him work out problems and struggles
and to provide the nurturance and support he needs, rather than
give up on him in times of difficulty.

Many foster children are moved at the request of foster parents, generally because the parents cannot deal with some aspect
of the child's behavior. So it is critical for foster parents to be aware
of their own limitations and be honest with themselves and agency
social workers before a child is placed in their home. In this
regard, the single most important thing that foster parents can do
is to be instrumental in reducing the number of moves that a foster
child might have to make during her time in care. Ongoing training, continuing education, and participation in foster parent support groups should always be utilized before asking that a child be
removed. Since these children already feel highly vulnerable and
to blame for the problems in their lives, their feelings of rejection
and abandonment will ultimately become irreversible if asked to
leave by a foster parent who lacks this commitment.

Helping the Child Prepare for
Termination of Parental Rights

A very difficult time in the life of many foster children comes when the biological parents' parental rights are terminated. Most often, this occurs when the biological parents continue the abusive and neglectful behavior that originally led to the child coming into foster care, when they maintain little or no visitation, and when they have shown to the court that they are not capable of changing to meet the child's needs. Before this happens, foster children often maintain the hope and belief that foster care will be temporary and that they will return home. But when parental rights of the biological parent are terminated, this hope is shattered and the child must move on to a new life in a new family. Foster parents can do a great deal to help the foster child at this very difficult time in her life.

One of the first things the foster parents must do is consider whether they want to become the adoptive parents or, for older children, to allow the child to remain in long-term foster care in their home. The foster parents must determine, as honestly as they can, whether they wish to make a long-term commitment to the child. If a stable relationship between the child and the foster parents has been developed and maintained for more than a year or so, foster parents who continue to provide a long-term commitment make the transition easier. The age of the child will have a major impact on the effect of this termination of parental rights and even how much awareness the child has. It is easier for very young children who have little or no awareness to have foster parents maintain a status quo and simply be their parents. For school-age or older children, sitting down and talking about these issues, about feelings of abandonment and rejection by the biological parents, and about the stable commitment within the new family will go a long way to reduce their fears after parental rights are terminated. Thus, if the foster family makes a long-term commitment through adoption or long-term foster care, the task of acceptance is much easier. This is not to say that the foster child will not engage in fantasy or maintain a longing to return to the birth family; but adjustment and acceptance are easier nonetheless.

Oftentimes, however, foster parents are not in a position to make a long-term commitment to their foster children when parental rights have been terminated. Foster care is not meant to be permanent, and most foster parents enter foster care with the understanding that it should be and will be temporary. Because of this, it is often expected that a different home will have to be found for the child once the court decides to take away parental rights. This new home will be a home for the future long-term commitment by a permanent and stable family. Foster parents can help the child make the transition to such a new home by talking openly with the child about his feelings, helping him feel that he is not "bad," and explaining that the pending move is for *permanence*. Remaining interested in the child and possibly visiting him after the change, like an aunt or uncle, will also help him with the transition from foster care to more permanent placement and possibly adoption. Finally, therapy might also be necessary to help the child with this transition.

8

Conclusion

B EING a foster parent is extremely hard work, but it is significantly rewarding when foster parents feel that they have
accomplished something of value. The most significant reward of
foster parenting comes from the relationship with a child who is
special and who improves while in their care. This reward tends to
make the work worthwhile, especially when foster parents are
recognized for the professional role they lead.

It is my belief, and the belief is shared by many others, that
foster parents should be better recognized as professionals and
financially and emotionally rewarded for it. Foster parents require
a great deal of training and a special sense of commitment to do
their "job" well, and society must learn to value that job if it hopes
to accumulate enough foster parents to do the job right.

In addition, there is a lot that foster parents can do to help
themselves. First is that they can promote and encourage participation in national, state, and local foster parent associations that
address these issues. Such associations can promote national and
local legislation to encourage the professional training and ongoing continuing education of foster parents and improve the status
of foster children. Such associations can offer training on a continuing basis and can set the standards for minimum training for
foster parents. Similarly, foster parent associations can develop
and maintain a set of ethical principles for foster parents and adopt
rules that members should follow to guarantee that minimum
standards of education and behavior are met.

Individual foster parents can also work with their local social
service agency staff to promote improved communication about

foster children, and they can encourage such staff to treat them in a more professional manner. By keeping written logs of behavioral progress, by informing staff of significant changes in the foster child's status or behavior, by taking the child to therapy and working with the therapist when necessary, and by continuing to promote the well-being and ongoing needs of the foster child, foster parents will force their community to treat them more professionally.

Finally, foster parents can make themselves more visible in their community. This encourages greater publicity about foster parenting and the needs of local foster children. Every year in one California county, foster parents work together to ensure that all foster children receive Christmas presents from shoppers in the local mall. This toy drive not only helps the foster children feel a sense of belonging to their community, it promotes and publicizes the needs of foster children and the need for more foster parents. By promoting themselves, foster parents can encourage more families to become foster families. This will ultimately lead to an overall improvement in the delivery of foster care to the children who need it most. If every foster parent reading this book recruited just one more family to become a foster family, there would be enough foster homes for all the children in need. Ultimately, that is our task, to guarantee the quality and quantity of service for the foster children in need. As foster parents become more professional, take their training and associations more seriously, work more closely with agency staff, and work to promote and publicize the needs of foster children and the benefits of foster parenting, we will go a long way toward helping the "children on consignment" in their care.

A Final Word

In this book I have written a great deal about the difficulties of being a foster child, the emotional needs of foster children, and the behaviors and problems of foster children. In conclusion, I'd like to mention the one ingredient that comes through every day in the work of foster parents and people in a community. That ingredient is *love*. When foster parents take someone into their family and help her feel "at home," give of their food and give of their hearts, they are sharing their love. Put in the simplest terms, foster children need all the love that they can get. By giving love openly and honestly and by giving of themselves, foster parents are sharing their special human qualities with those most in need—the abused and neglected children of our society. By following through on this love with *commitment*, foster parents say to the children that they are important and that the world is a safe and caring place. If they do nothing else than this, foster parents have given the most important item they can, a share of their human will.

Keep giving, and enjoy your special place in the hearts of the children you serve.

Index

About the Author

PHILIP STAHL received his doctorate in education from the University of Michigan. While in Michigan, he was a consultant for a variety of social service agencies. During that time, he worked with and evaluated over a thousand foster children, foster families, and biological parents. In that work, he discovered that there was a need for foster parents to be better trained and to be treated more professionally. This book is his contribution to that process. Currently, Dr. Stahl is in private practice in Dublin, California, where he continues his association with foster families and social service agencies.